Callister Press

Justice Waits

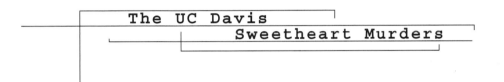

The UC Davis
Sweetheart Murders

Joel Davis

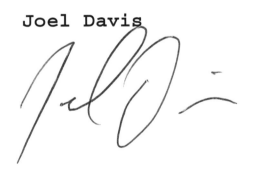

A portion of any profits will be donated to charities
designated by the Gonsalves and Riggins families.

Printed on acid-free paper in the United States by Sheridan Books, Inc.

Cover and book design by Jay Leek at Six Finger Design
with contributions from Joel Davis, David Forster and John Hershey

Production by Joel Davis, John Hershey and Jay Leek

Editing by Jeff Aberbach, Anna Davis, Kelly Johnson Davis, Kathi Denny,
David Forster, John Hershey, Carolyn Ralston, Frances Sackett and
Charles Winkler

ISBN 0-9741603-0-X

www.justicewaits.com

*To my wife, Kelly, a steel magnolia (in the fine tradition
of Kate Riggins) who never blinked. To the Riggins and Gonsalves
families, who bravely backed this project from the start ...
And to all the innocent people affected by this extraordinary case.*

John and Sabrina — Sabrina and John
Hand in hand walking into the fog.
Encountering darkness there in the night...
But darkness cannot overcome the pure light.

— Marge Wellings

Pleased to meet you
Hope you guessed my name
But what's puzzling you
Is the nature of my game

— Keith Richards/Mick Jagger

Contents

Foreword

It was the summer of 2000. I was working from my office in San Francisco's Transamerica Pyramid building when I got a call from one of my best friends, Dan Ariola. Dan asked me if I remembered a Joel Davis from high school. Vague visions of a tall, lanky, dark-haired, tobacco-chewing, mediocre basketball player came to mind. I mumbled something about didn't he play basketball with Dan. Dan confirmed that was the same Joel whom he had last seen 20 years ago on the high school basketball court, and that out of the blue he had just gotten a call from Joel. Dan said, "You won't believe what he wants to do."

What Joel wanted was to write a book about the abduction and murders of John Riggins and Sabrina Gonsalves, two 18-year-old college freshmen sweethearts. Their murders, in December 1980, remain the most brutal crime to afflict Davis, Calif., a theretofore innocent, bucolic college town 10 miles west of the state capital in Sacramento. John had been one of my two best friends. My other best friend, Scott Hill, and I had known John since third grade. Our three birthdays were all within two weeks of one another and we had spent our adolescence competing and ganging up on one another. As memories, both good and bad, came flooding back, I was both wary and intrigued by what Joel wanted to do.

I was wary because of the families involved. Dan told me that Joel needed an introduction to Kate Riggins, John's mother. I have gotten to know the Riggins family quite well after that dreadful, foggy December night, and often visited John's parents at their home along the California coast. The painful reopening of wounds from 20 years ago was nothing to take lightly. While Joel and I shared the same high school, I didn't really know him and I certainly wasn't about to introduce him to Kate Riggins without knowing more about his motives and abilities. Moreover, I was sure the families would not want a sensationalized Hollywood-like account of the case. I suspected they would not want John and Sabrina to be portrayed as unrealistically perfect angels, nor hapless victims. While guarded, I was also very much intrigued by the thought of a fresh set of eyes on a dormant, mostly forgotten cold case.

Years ago, I had fantasized about spending a year to sift through all the evidence to see what I might discover. How could I be sure every lead had been uncovered and pursued? Like some tidy TV show, what if a new set of eyes could find the killer(s) and finally bring justice to the families?

I met Joel, and in contrast to my vague recollections from high school, I was impressed by his credentials (editor of his college paper, master's degree from Columbia University, newspaper reporter and columnist, freelance writer, college journalism instructor), read his writing samples and grew confident that he meant to undertake a serious and sober investigation of the case. I finally reached for the phone to call Kate Riggins and introduce her to Joel, not knowing what, if any good, would come from his efforts.

The writing of this book has been more than Joel could ever have imagined. To his own surprise, he has become a part of the story, a participatory journalist, not just a chronicler of events. Sadly, this case continues to take its toll. Since our first conversation in mid-2000, Joel has been diagnosed with Parkinson's disease. A one-year project has turned into five years and counting. Through it all, Joel traveled from courthouse to courthouse,sifting through case files while interviewing key people in this story. He has withstood intimidation and tears and soldiered on in a textbook example of investigative journalism. The result of his heroic efforts, along with those of the investigators and district attorneys office, is a dormant case that has become very much alive. And while justice still waits, there is fresh hope again that it may finally be served.

— John Hershey
May 2005

Preface

I went to junior high and high school with John Riggins. I did not know him well. I knew him more through osmosis, via common friends with an interest in sports. At best we might have shared a nod at the grocery store, a "hey" on the sports fields of Davis. I definitely remember the red hair. I never met Sabrina Gonsalves. But I know her now, or at least I think I do.

But I did know John Riggins well enough to be among the shocked and bewildered when he and Sabrina Gonsalves were kidnapped in my hometown and brutally murdered the weekend of my 18th birthday.

I left Davis but this case never left me.

"Why?"

Everyone from members of John and Sabrina's families to the detectives involved to some of the people who were arrested for these heinous murders asked me a variation of the same question when I told them about this project back in the summer of 2000.

"Why write about a 20-year-old murder?"

"Why write about an open case?"

"Why write a story that has no ending?"

It's simple, really. Or...it was simple. Everything about my life, my plans, my vision, was simple in 2000. There have been many times since that I asked myself why. Be careful what you wish for. This book took a lot of blood, sweat, toil, tears and calling in favors I can never repay. I was as humbled at finishing it as I was cocksure at starting it.

Nothing from pestering investigators and attorneys who have difficult jobs to do to chasing down court documents all over creation came easy. And looking back, maybe that's how it was meant to be. Throw in the rapid onset of a devastating disease I hardly heard of when I started this tome to one that rudely awakens me each morning feeling like a tire that has a little less tread than the day before, and the whole endeavor has been a little bit like herding feral cats.

But back to the book. I meant to finish it and I have. At the risk of being immodest, I like it. There were times during this project when I didn't much like me, some of the key people involved, me again, but I was, in some very peculiar ways that may very well be fodder for another book at another time, given critical distance from it on more than one occasion, not always by choice. And despite suggestions to fix this and eliminate that, despite having nine very capable editors go over it with very capable eyes and reactions that were all over the lot, every time I came back to it I came to the conclusion that the person I most needed to believe in was ... me. There are some things here that have stayed here because of nothing more than stubbornness from a stubborn writer.

I wrote this book for my generation, for the people who, like me, were around when this happened and, to quote a very good dentist friend of mine, found these murders to be "a pretty f----d-up thing to happen to our town during our senior year." Kind of a blunt assessment, but hard to argue with it, Dr. G.

But back to the best-laid plans here: I took this project on as a combination of my curiosity as a journalist and someone who felt violated along with the rest of the small college town during that ominous foggy weekend. But mostly out of curiosity. In a way, it was kind of selfish.

I finished it some five years later with my curiosity satiated, with a sense of satisfaction and achievement for telling a story that needed to be told, for stirring a pot that needed to be stirred, even if my spoon was not always welcome in the pot. Depending on whom you talk to, I helped get this case solved.

But I cannot help but be bothered still by the fact that anything that was done or not done by me could get around, hide or overcome the fact that two terrific kids (funny how I now refer to people older than I was when this happened as ... kids) died brutal, savage deaths, amazingly promising lives literally cut short before so much promise could be fulfilled.

Once, on the anniversary of the murders, John's mother, Kate, one of my many heroes here, confided after some back-and-forth remembrances, "What's the difference...They're still dead." That simple but telling line from a parent who has endured an anguish that I can only write about and not feel, sticks with me.

I knew this would be an unusual case. I just didn't realize how unusual: Every answer seemed to come with at least two more questions. One step forward, two steps back, it often seemed. Some of what you will read is my interpretation of things: My hometown (which may appear to be a little picked on at times, but Davis, I love you more often than not, I really do), my generation, my relationship with the victims' families and the principal people involved.

This book, which I figured would take about a year to write, evolved into a complex and highly sensitive project. Never did I imagine that this case would take such dramatic turns when I started looking into it. I also never intended to be part of the story. Journalists are meant to be observers, not participants. I'm not particularly fond of first-person journalism; you're not, unless you are my mom, here to read about me. But over time it became obvious that the "I" would be necessary. I nevertheless looked at my role here as a conduit of sorts: investigate and report what happened since Dec. 20, 1980.

A hell of a lot happened.

— Joel Davis
May 2005

1
Joker Joe

*"...And still the men chatted pleasantly, and smiled. Was it possible
they heard not? Almighty God!—no, no? They heard!—they suspected!—
they knew!—they were making a mockery of my horror!—this I thought,
and this I think. But anything was better than this agony!"*

— Edgar Allan Poe ("The Telltale Heart")

By all accounts, Joseph Hirschfield had made a good life for himself. At
the age of 47, he had a pretty new wife, two cars, and clear title on 2 1/2
rain-kissed acres in Beavercreek, Ore., a heavenly burg tucked away on the
outskirts of Portland. Sheep and dogs roamed the postcard-perfect property
on Schuebel Lane, a gravel road that emited soothing pops and crunches
under moving tires and feet. Sure, Joe lived in a triple-wide, but it was a nice,
ranch-style model adjacent to a cavernous 3,000-square-foot barn/shop
where Joe liked to tinker.

A well-paid mechanic for a local Cadillac dealership who taught scuba
diving on the side, Joe had a knack for computers and had even gone back
to school to learn more about them, perhaps to become an IT administrator.
He was known in various chatrooms and e-mail addresses as "Joker Joe" —
even ran his own Web site at one time. A gourmet cook, ladies man, flirt and
a prankster, Joe was generous, handsome, athletic, well-liked by the few people he let know him well and he often repaired things gratis for friends and
people in need. He was also handy with a knife, and occasionally used one
to butcher sheep on his small spread, a skill he picked up as a youth on the
family farm in Colusa County, north of Sacramento, Calif. Joe could slice an
animal's throat with a swift, clean cut.

The only thing unusual about Joe is that he tended to keep to himself, living in an insular world with his wife, Lana, a medical transcriber, and their
two Rottweillers. He was a remote man in a remote community. "They acted

Joe and Lana Hirschfield at their wedding.
Lana Hirschfield

strange," a neighbor said. "They were loners. Joe never talked to me — and I lived across the street from him for 11 years."

Other than a smattering of traffic violations and small-claims cases, Joker Joe was a model citizen in his 20 years in the greater Portland area, most of them in Beavercreek. He was not known to law enforcement in a region where even the smallest skirmish with the authorities is remembered. Remarried after divorcing his second wife in the mid-1990s, he seemingly had a bright future when detectives from Sacramento County knocked on his door Nov. 19, 2002. Joe, his wife told them, was at work. She then phoned her husband. "There are two detectives from Sacramento who want to talk to you about your brother," she said to the man she often described as "the most perfect, loving, wonderful husband."

In 1980, the detectives had recently learned, Joe lived in Rancho Cordova, just a few miles from the ravine where John Riggins and Sabrina Gonsalves were found dead on Dec. 22, 1980, in the brutal UC Davis sweetheart murders. There was nothing connecting him to the grisly slayings. But Joker Joe visibly shook in his mechanic's jumper at Kuni Cadillac in Beaverton as detectives told him about new leads in the case and the names Riggins and Gonsalves. Even though it was mid-November, sweat poured out of him. Joe was clammy. Joe knew something. Something that ate away at his conscience and had nibbled on his soul for most of his adult life. Now the joke was on the joker. Joe was so rattled he left work early. *"My brother...,"* Joe muttered to a co-worker as he set down his tools, *"is in big trouble for something that* _happened years ago..._"

Joe was a part of a multistate detective blitz in which Hirschfield family members were confronted, including a mother in failing health who nearly went into shock when she heard her oldest was a murder suspect. The following morning, after the Sacramento detectives left Beavercreek, Joker Joe said goodbye to his wife, left his triple-wide, and headed, as he always did on workdays, to fetch his car. But instead of driving his 1994 Subaru to work, he guided it into the barn and closed the door behind him. In the same car he took on his honeymoon, Joe methodically attached a hose from the car's exhaust pipe to its interior. He climbed inside and rolled up the windows. He started the engine and took long, deep breaths. He died quietly, and alone. His wife found him when she went into the barn to feed the sheep – the same barn where Joe may have had flashbacks every time he slit an animal's throat. Beside him lay a brief note addressed to her that made reference to the murders.

It said, "It's only a matter of time before they find my DNA, too."

2
Fog

The flu raced through Davis on Saturday, Dec. 20, 1980, and Kate and Dick Riggins still had a touch of it. Even though they were both a bit sick, even though it was so foggy that you could not see your neighbor's house, the practical orthopedic surgeon and his vibrant wife, both 45, were determined to celebrate their wedding anniversary, if only to slip out for an hour to the one place in the sleepy college town with a halfway-decent steak.

They drove past houses invisible save for the holiday lights suspended in the early evening winter's mist, a hauntingly beautiful contrast that is Davis' signature around the holidays. Dr. and Mrs. Riggins carefully navigated their modest blue Honda Civic — in Davis you flaunt intelligence, not possessions — to A.J. Bumps restaurant on G Street in the center of town about a mile away.

God, it was foggy. If there's one thing locals remember about this short day and long night, the weekend of the winter solstice, it was the blinding, worse-than-usual tule fog, a bone-chilling fog that soaks through a sweater or slides up a pant leg, a fog so dense that it muffles sound, envelopes the face in a dewy emulsion. The fog this day even grounded the starlings in the trees outside the steak house, the huddled birds squawking angrily through the gray mist at Kate and Dick as they sauntered past.

Prior to heading to Bumps, as it was known, the Rigginses took an afternoon nap to fight off the flu. During their rest, their oldest child, John, an athletic, redheaded University of California Davis freshman who still lived at home, padded into his parents' bedroom in a mild panic, uncharacteristic for the happy-go-lucky 18-year-old.

John Harold Riggins had just finished his finals earlier that Saturday at UC Davis, a demanding, no-nonsense university, the type of school that has finals on Saturdays. And like most college freshmen, John Riggins agonized over a major. He wondered whether he should stick with engineering or switch to his surgeon-father's career.

"I've been thinking about it, and I think I'm going to make a change," he told his parents as he hovered over their bed. "I think I'll change to pre-med."

Sure that John had plenty of time in the years ahead to reconsider, Kate and Dick tried to ease John's restless mind.

"Oh, John," they countered. "Just stick with this."

Just stick with this.

On the afternoon of Dec. 20, 1980, on their 22nd wedding anniversary of all days, these were the last words Kate and Dick Riggins would speak to their first child, the last time they would look at his compact athletic body, his expressive, freckled face and his beautiful thatch of red hair.

From now on, Dec. 20 would be an unforgettable day for all the wrong reasons.

————

Early the next day, in a condominium a half-mile from the Riggins' West Davis home, a light and fan were on. Usually a light illuminating a bathroom with the fan whirring is comforting, a routine tonic in the daily ritual, the soothing white noise of the first to arise.

In the condo of sisters and UC Davis students Andrea Marie Gonsalves and Sabrina Marie Gonsalves, both devout Catholics, on the foggy, rainy, dismal Sunday morning of Dec. 21, 1980, it was the sign of something terribly wrong.

Andrea, the older, more outgoing sister, also had a touch of the flu and had gone to bed early the night before. She left the light and fan on for her responsible, quiet sibling Sabrina. Pretty, lithe and athletic, Sabrina, 18, was out with her equally responsible boyfriend, John Riggins, Saturday night.

Sabrina and John had failed to show up to a surprise birthday party for Andrea that the third Gonsalves sister, Terese, hosted on Saturday night in her West Davis apartment. While this was out of character, Andrea figured they stayed late working as ushers at a local children's performance of "The Nutcracker" at the Veterans Memorial Center a mile away. Or being big Beatles fans, they perhaps headed over to the Cinema 2 to see a special hastily arranged showing of "The Magical Mystery Tour" in the wake of John Lennon's assassination 10 days earlier.

Finals, party, "Nutcracker," Beatles, Christmas. Whatever. It was a busy day during a busy time of year. Who knew where John and Sabrina might have gone?

Andrea, whose last words to Sabrina were an admonishment that she not hoard for John's family all the best Christmas cookies the sisters baked because they could not afford to buy gifts, flipped the light and fan on before she drifted off to sleep, weak from illness. Like a slap in the face, the fan and light were still on when Andrea woke up Sunday morning.

Sabrina never had a chance to turn them off.

Joel Davis

8

Fog

3
Family Business

On Dec. 20, 1980, in Carson City, Nev., a three-hour drive and a world away from Davis, it was not foggy.

Here, Suellen Brifman, a pretty, chatty former prison counselor, and David Hunt, a hardened lifelong criminal buff from prison weightlifting, met to marry at the Sunset wedding chapel, known for brisk nuptials. Suellen, still married to another man, seemed willing to do anything for her soft-spoken outlaw lover.

Suellen and Hunt, both 36, met in 1978 after Hunt's arrest and subsequent parole-violation imprisonment for stealing sheets from a Holiday Inn in San Jose. Drawn to Hunt's macho ways, and thinking she could rehabilitate him, that they could somehow have a life together, she swiftly fell in love with him.

Accompanying Hunt to Carson City was his former San Quentin Prison cell mate, his "road dog," Richard Thompson. Both had long arrest records, both were familiar with weapons. A disguised, armed Hunt had helped break Thompson out of San Quentin during a daring escape a month earlier, after which they went on a multistate crime spree in the Pacific Northwest. They were wanted in California and had been living as fugitives under assumed names in a Phoenix, Ariz., barrio.

Hunt's half-brother, Gerald Gallego, 34, whom Hunt had revered since their troubled upbringing in Sacramento, had recently been arrested and jailed for the brutal sex-slave murder-kidnappings of two attractive Sacramento State University sweethearts in November. Hunt had been fiercely protective of his younger brother since the two were boys in a broken home in Sacramento. When he learned Gallego was wanted for the murders, he phoned Gallego's mother-in law, asking if he could do anything to help.

On Dec. 18, the night before traveling from Phoenix to Carson City, Hunt and Thompson engaged in a bizarre blood-bonding ritual in which Thompson got drunk and acted belligerent, out of character for a man who, despite his criminal lifestyle, was generally low-key. Hunt cut their wrists and commingled their blood in some sort of weird pact.

Accompanying Hunt and Thompson from Phoenix to Carson City were Thompson's wife, Valerie, and Bill Lansing, a scruffy Phoenix neighbor of Hunt's who admired Hunt's macho outlaw lifestyle. A wannabe. They rumbled toward Carson City in a rusty 1965 Dodge van that contained, among other things, knives and disguises.

Meanwhile, with her 11-year-old daughter and two dogs and up to seven cats in tow, Suellen on Dec. 19 somehow managed to navigate a rental van to Carson City – passing through Davis along the way – from her Menlo Park, Calif., home. She met Hunt and the others at the Carson City Motel 6, where two rooms were reserved under false names. After the brief, bigamous afternoon wedding ceremony the next day, Dec. 20, Lansing, the newcomer in the group, was dropped off at a casino by his new friends about 4 p.m.

"We have," Hunt told him, "family business to take care of."

4
Davis
- - - - - - - - - - - - -

*"My dad did not want me to go to Berkeley, he decided it was unsafe.
He was overseas in Germany at the time, and he needed to know that
his girls would be safe. This is what's such an irony."*

— Andrea Gonsalves

It was a bucolic college town in 1980. It is a sophisticated university city
now.

But there is no mistaking Davis, aka the City of All Things Right and Relevant, Volvoville, the Reality-Free Zone, Berkeley with a Haircut.

Davis is a fascinating and perplexing city, a contradiction by the causeway. The former Davisville is educated, idyllic, affluent, progressive, agrarian,
petty, strong, vulnerable, NIMBY, diverse on the one hand, lily white on the
other, leafy and wonderful. It has lush parks (about two dozen, not counting the scores of quasi-parks known as greenbelts) in every neighborhood;
charming, red, double-decker London buses that stylishly shuttle students
around town; a renowned farmers market; and highly regarded public schools
where, as in the mythical Lake Wobegone, "The children are all above average." Its colorful boutiques and ethnic eateries have transformed Davis into
an upscale shopping destination, a cow town no more.

Davis is a desirable community almost in spite of itself. It can be unbear-
ably hot in the summer, damp, foggy and cold in the winter. It has a tediously
flat terrain and is hell for seasonal allergy sufferers. Its tap water is nearly
undrinkable. Insects crowd the arid summer air as crop harvests and burn-
ings dirty it. To view Davis' layout from one of the many overpasses ringing
the city is to be underwhelmed.

Yet Davis is the second-most-educated city in the country (behind Chapel
Hill, N.C.), and is rapidly becoming one of the most exclusive and affluent
university towns on the West Coast. Its tree-lined, older neighborhoods in
the shadows of the burgeoning university lend an Ivy League flavor. Stroll

the campus on a leafy fall afternoon or the downtown farmers market on a starry night fanned by the delta breeze and you will be charmed.

The community and its sprawling University of California campus have spawned innovations in solar energy, recycling, agriculture, housing, medicine, community planning and transportation. Expect more innovation and more affluence: UC Davis' schools of medicine, management and law have positioned the university ideally for stem cell funding and research.

A lot of big ideas come out of a place that can be small-minded. Davis residents have been cited or chided for smoking outside in public places, snoring too loudly, using leaf blowers, and painting their house the wrong color. Police are even known to slap wobbly bicyclists with "BWIs" — tickets for bicycling while intoxicated — on slow nights.

Davis has declared itself nuclear-free (from what is not quite clear) and has spent public money for a tunnel for toads to safely cross a road. There's no proof the toads prefer this to the more reckless routes, but stranger things have been done in town, such as the time artist-Mayor Julie Partansky advocated that a city police officer dress up as a fruit or vegetable to blend in while serving as a farmers market crossing guard.

The city's liberal elitism is renowned, resented and somewhat misleading. Davis' school lunches are closely monitored for nutritional value. More than 90 percent of the mothers breast-feed their newborns. It is home to the Hillary Rodham Clinton fan club as well as organizations dedicated to fighting noise pollution and artificial light blocking the stars at night. Davis has both a welcoming and gated-community feel. The city seems progressive in everything but race relations — there have been several disturbing if isolated racial incidents in the last several years — and growth. Davis has been slow to respond to traffic and housing needs. Its famed public school system, a reputation symbiotically tied to involved/demanding parents as much as involved/demanding teachers, has pushed housing costs out of reach for most. Among those squeezed out are many who grew up in Davis and, ironically, some of the very teachers whose stellar reputations help drive up the prices to begin with. The average price of a house in Davis is now well over $500,000.

"We're about as liberal as a bunch of white people living in $800,000 houses who sit around the pool talking about how liberal we are," cracked longtime Davis Enterprise columnist Bob Dunning, who has been sagely writing about Davis for more than three decades. (Dunning, like me a native son, regularly mocks the city, much to its inhabitants' secret delight; most locals, to their credit, are good-natured enough to take part in the self-deprecation.)

Davis nevertheless has responsible, compassionate people and an unrivaled sense of community. It is the rare sort of town where meals for the poor draw more volunteers than downtrodden diners. It is a cheerful, friendly city, rising to the occasion in troubled times. Both the Riggins and Gonsalves families remain deeply touched by the outpouring of support after John and Sabrina were, in Kate Riggins' inimitable words, "destroyed."

The Davis of Dec. 20, 1980, the date that made John and Sabrina famous for all the wrong reasons, is my Davis, the Davis I know like a sibling. It had a population of 36,640 and was more of an intellectual Mayberry than the hectic, more vibrant, even impersonal, university city of 65,000-plus it has become. Downtown Davis in 1980 was mostly locally owned businesses that were usually shuttered on nights and weekends. Now bustling, the city has in recent years unfurled the corporate welcome mat for Borders Books, The Gap, Starbucks and Tower Records, among others. In 1980, by contrast, the local merchant ruled. You bought your Christmas gifts at Winger's department store, your Hush Puppies at H&C Shoes, your baseball mitt at the Davis Sport Shop, your vinyl records at Barney's, your prom duds at Tingus Menswear, your medicine and greeting cards at Quessenberry's, maybe your groceries at the funky State Market.

The cause du jour in 1980 was gay rights amid the usual litany of sub-controversies, including considerable consternation over what color to paint a large iron bike sculpture on Russell Boulevard. More than 400 residents crowded a public meeting in January to discuss Proposition A, a local gay rights ordinance in the city. Six months of typical Davis hand-wringing and legal wrangles over the issue followed, capped by a rally at city hall *against* Proposition A. In another sign of the city's stealthy conservative streak, Davis voters thumped the measure by a 2-1 margin.

When Davis Enterprise editors met at the end of 1980 to pick a top story, gay rights and its half-year saga was the clear choice. That is until John and Sabrina were found murdered on Dec. 22. The brutal slayings were — and remain — the most shocking crime in city history,[1] the newspaper's obvious choice for Top Story of 1980. (And again in 1981 and 1989.)

Though I was having too much senior-year fun at Davis High to really notice, it was, had I bothered to take off my rose-colored shades, a terrible time. Nationally, it was the last year of Jimmy Carter's failed presidency that

---

[1] Also considered Davis' most shocking crimes: The 1972 McFarland murder-suicide in which a UC Davis professor killed his wife and three children before torching his Davis home; the 1983 stabbing death of Thong Hy Huynh, an Asian student who died on the Davis High School campus in a racially motivated attack; and the 1992 murder of Holmes Junior High student Andrew Mockus, who was pushed into the side of a moving train by fellow teens after being beaten and robbed of $2.

shakily segued into a slow-starting Reagan reign; inflation was high; an energy crisis made for long lines at the pump (and a mandatory home energy-conservation ordinance in Davis); and the U.S. botched a rescue attempt of the U.S. hostages in Iran. John Lennon, whom John Riggins worshipped, and Anwar Sadat were killed by assassins' bullets, President Reagan and Pope John Paul II almost were. On Nov. 21, 1980, a fire at the MGM Grand hotel in Las Vegas killed 87.

The national pastime, baseball, opened the season with a 60-day strike. In the spring of 1981 a strange and insidious new disease affecting mainly gay men in the United States was detected. It would be called AIDS. It was officially recognized by the Centers for Disease Control on Friday, June 5 – the day the Class of '81, my class, graduated from Davis High.

It was no better closer to home. John and Sabrina weren't even the *first* UC Davis sweethearts to be killed in 1980: Robin Ann Ehlman, 20, and her boyfriend, John Kevin Manville, 25, were gunned down March 4 at the Castilian Apartments in West Davis. (Ehlman's ex-boyfriend, Daniel Wehner, 27, pleaded guilty to the murders.) Also in the news was Luis Rodriguez, on trial for killing two CHP officers on a foggy morning in nearby West Sacramento in 1978, as well as the drug-overdose suicide of Sacramento "Vampire Killer" Richard Chase, who drank the blood of some of his six murder victims.

The city even had its squeaky-clean image tarnished by a rat infestation, appointing Councilman Jerry Adler (a Riggins family friend who continues to help with this case) to oversee a rat-extermination campaign. In the spring of 1981, Ellen Hansen and Steve Haertle, both 20 – like John and Sabrina, model kids – were shot by "Trailside Killer" David Carpenter during a hike in the Santa Cruz Mountains. Hansen died in the attack; Haertle survived and testified against Carpenter, who was convicted and is on Death Row. In a big city, things like that are taken in stride. In Davis, where, the thinking goes, a criminal may take your bicycle but not your life, they are shocking.

"My dad did not want me to go to Berkeley, he decided it was unsafe," Sabrina's sister/roommate Andrea noted. "He looked into all the UC systems – they were all unsafe compared to Davis. He was overseas in Germany at the time, and he needed to know that his girls would be safe. This is what's such an irony."

And as wonderful as John and Sabrina were, the fact that their last day alive began in Davis is one of many things that makes this case amazing. Perhaps it's the most extraordinary thing. Davis cares, Davis frets. So when

Davis suffers a setback, a real setback, not just hand-wringing over leaf blowers, bicycle sculptures and the night sky, it is keenly felt and not easily forgotten. For all its quirks Davis is a special place. To grow up there is to come of age in a sort of children's Eden, brimming with scores of city-sponsored activities during long, carefree summer days spent in city parks and swimming pools, happily accessible by bike. Most people who grew up in Davis feel blessed and cursed for coming of age in a city that is both enriching and overly sheltered.

John and Sabrina, unfortunately, never got to make this assessment.

5
That Hair

John Riggins was all over the place when he lived in Davis, or it least his brilliant shock of red hair made you think he was. That red hair certainly made me think I knew John Riggins better than I did.

It caught the notice of area newspaper photographers, who tended to snap his picture more than other athletes. And it captured the heart of Sabrina and the attention of other dark-haired Gonsalves women, who to this day wistfully note, "He had the most *beautiful* red hair."

That hair. Guys' hairstyles in the bell-bottomed 1970s/early 1980s were awkward blends of the short styles to come and the long styles that were, yet John Riggins pulled it off. His hair was his calling card since he was a tot, something instantly recognizable on the streets and playgrounds of Davis, where John Riggins was often seen pedaling along his newspaper route from blocks away, his compact, sun-burn-prone legs pumping like pistons, his neck holding up a hefty sack of Sacramento Bees.

"It was amazing," John's mother, Kate Riggins, herself a handsome redhead who bears a strong resemblance to her oldest child, said in her pecan pie-sweet Southern drawl. "People were always wanting to touch him." That's if he would sit still long enough to be touched. As a toddler, little John bubbled with curiosity, a freckled dynamo who nimbly displayed his athleticism on trees, jungle gyms and anything else he could climb. "He wasn't a clinger," Kate recalled. "He was very independent. And competitive. You'd go to a playground and he was in there immediately doing everything you could do. But if you said, 'John, it's time to come' — he'd come."

Adventuresome. Competitive. But mindful, considerate and fiercely protective. It was a pattern that continued until the day John Riggins died. His mother, Cecelia "Kate" Mahood, grew up in Oakridge, Tenn., where she was the doted-on only child of an attorney (and college baseball star) father and schoolteacher mother. It was at the Duke School of Medicine that Kate, studying to be a dietitian, met Richard "Dick" Riggins, a compact, sturdily

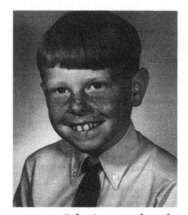

John in second grade.
Kate Riggins

built, bow-tie-wearing, no-nonsense native Floridian (John had his mom's face and his dad's body) born to a Canadian mother who was a nurse, and a chemist father from New Jersey.

With Dick in medical school, they had little money and lived in the graduate dorms. In 1958 when both were 23, they wed on the now-bittersweet date of Dec. 20. Dick's demanding schedule necessitated getting married in December during some rare time off.

John Riggins was born Jan. 18, 1962, into a world chilled by the Cold War and a country bubbling in racial turmoil. On the day Kate, then 27, gave birth to her first child at Duke University Hospital in Durham, N.C., Southern University was closed due to racial tension, the U.S. performed a nuclear test in Nevada, and the Army began spraying foliage in Vietnam with Agent Orange to reveal Viet Cong guerrillas.

Kate worked as a clinical dietitian up until John's birth. Dick's internship and residencies at hospitals in Williamson, W. Va., Washington, D.C., and the National Institutes of Health in Bethesda, Md., included a two-year public health residency that counted toward what was in those years mandatory military service for physicians. It was also during this time that Dick decided he'd like to be an orthopedic surgeon because in orthopedics the patient usually gets better.

He was accepted into a prestigious three-year orthopedics program at Campbell Clinic in Memphis, Tenn. It was here that the younger Riggins

**Robert, Carrie and John Riggins in the
family's 1980 Christmas card photo.**

Kate Riggins

children, Carrie and Robert, were born. Finished with Campbell, Dick Riggins shuttled his young family back to his native Florida, where he took over the practice of a friend from his Duke days who had been summoned by the Air Force for medical duty.

The Rigginses found West Palm Beach, Fla., a bit of an aging backwater with a shaky school, a less than idyllic place to raise a family. When John came home from first grade and counted to four with a backwoods cadence of "One-two-three...fo'!" the family decided to relocate somewhere with a stronger school system. Davis was ideal. Dick moved his family to the city in 1969, one of the community's most bountiful years for drawing UC Davis talent as the university expanded.

The Rigginses migrated to Davis via Dick's association with Dr. Paul Lipscomb, a highly regarded orthopedic surgeon who headed the fledgling UC Davis orthopedics department. Just as they were formative years for Davis, the 1970s were formative years for the Rigginses. While Dick's career prospered and Kate became a fixture in volunteer circles (the couple, incidentally, bear a striking resemblance to the lead parents on "That 70s Show"— right down to both mothers' cackling laughs), the children were regulars in the Davis parks and recreation programs.

Despite being a family headed by a surgeon of local renown, the Rigginses did not flaunt it. They drove practical cars and did not spoil the kids: the Gonsalves girls and John's friends say he rarely had much spending money in high school and college because it was up to him to earn it; he once paid back a $3 loan to Andrea Gonsalves for a movie ticket in nickels and pennies. "I'm sorry for the change, but it's all I had," John says in a note Andrea Gonsalves treasures in a scrapbook.

The Rigginses lived on leafy Bucknell Drive (home of the annual "Bucknell Bowl" football game between the Riggins boys and the Frenz brothers across the street) in a large but simple Streng house, functional abodes in older Davis that are still coveted for their sturdiness. But there is more to the Rigginses than meets the eye, namely a Southern eccentricity that stood out inside their two-story home.

The rooms were all different colors, which, even in the funky 1970s, was unusual. Amid the house's crazy color scheme was an antique wooden carousel horse that served as the home's Christmas tree and backdrop for pictures, including John's prom portrait.

The Riggins kids were good kids, low-maintenance, a nice luck of the draw in a town where some of the wildest kids hailed from some of the most accomplished families. That's not to say John didn't have his faults and quirks. After he was killed, the media portrayed John as a responsible, church-going athlete/scholar, a sort of adored pied piper to the children he looked after in city recreation programs. While this isn't necessarily untrue – kids did have a strong bond to him and he was a beloved natural-born leader to both children (even if he accidentally once led them into a UC Davis fraternity house wallpapered with centerfolds) and his peers, there's more to John Riggins that makes him, well, human.

John loved cranking up rock 'n' roll. Though he eschewed the truly edgy stuff of his day, punk, he adored the bombast of the Who and Lynyrd Skynrd. While still in high school he boldly snuck into hot tubs with friends at college apartment complexes. Though he avoided drugs entirely and alcohol most of the time, he knocked back the occasional beer with his high school and college buddies: he had scheduled a beer-tasting with two of them, John Hershey and Scott Hill, the weekend he died, but canceled at the last minute because he wanted to accompany Sabrina to her sister's surprise party. "We didn't see much of John after he hooked up with Sabrina," recalled Dan Ariola, one of John's baseball teammates and now a championship-winning coach of the Davis High baseball team.

Helping and leading children came naturally to John, but his male friends and brother Robert point out that he also considered his parks and recreation job a way to make money for pizza, movies and records. He attended Episcopal Church of St. Martin, but not necessarily on his own volition. "My parents I'm sure will argue with me, but going to church and all was very forced," Carrie noted.

John got under Carrie's skin with surgical precision. Often enlisting his little brother's help, John conspired to pick on his sister often enough that Kate and Dick purchased the now-infamous Chevy van at least in part because it had expansive bench seats to avert backseat battles. In fact, the two fought over who got to use the van the Saturday night John was kidnapped: Carrie "lost," pedaling her bicycle through the eerie fog to her boyfriend's house.

"I can look at all his positive attributes now, but growing up I probably thought he was a typical big brother, and he would take the car when I wanted it," Carrie, two years younger than John, said. "He would also play his music really loud in the morning and wake me up."

Robert, too, recalled all sides of his brother. "He could be the manipulative older sibling. He and I would gang up on Carrie and he would come up with some plan and I would follow it," he said. "But he was a great older brother. We did a lot together, especially sports. He wouldn't mind me tagging along most of the time, even though he got needled from these other guys for bringing the little brother along."

From my delinquent universe, I categorized John Riggins as something of a jock/nerd. A harsh assessment, but he hung out with basketball teammates of mine whose idea of wild times was staying up late to watch "Saturday Night Live." At Davis High there were athlete-partyers — party vikings by today's standards, it being the digest first/worry later universe of the 1970s and early 1980s. Marijuana, cocaine and hallucinogenics were easily found, and it was easy to slip into UC Davis fraternity parties. You could, if you wanted to, grow up fast.

Then there were athlete-scholars who toed the line. John definitely ran with the latter crowd. But John, handsome in a wholesome Ron Howard/Boris Becker way (the resemblance to Becker is uncanny), was very up-to-speed on one thing:

Girls.

Cute, classy girls. And, with his clean good looks, manners ("he had the best manners," Sabrina's mother, Kim Gonsalves, said), and athleticism, John Riggins could attract girls. He would have been quite popular with the Davis High ladies had he not been, in his sister's words, "a slow mover." And while he may have been bashful around girls, John Riggins did like, look at and talk about them. He ogled jiggly Elvis movies and the ribald "Benny Hill Show." He tacked the iconic 1970s Farrah Fawcett swimsuit poster on his red bedroom wall. While Sabrina was his first real girlfriend, John did have a quasi-girlfriend in England, and Carrie once walked in on him in a lip-lock with her best friend, Renee Dorf, one of the prettiest, smartest girl-next-door types at Davis High. "I knew the real reason Renee came over to the house," Carrie said, laughing.

He escorted to the senior prom an attractive dark-haired sophomore gymnast who was eventually a Davis High homecoming queen. He double-dated with another shy jock/scholarly type, David Hartzell, who remembers the occasion well.

"John and I wanted to do something special, something out of the mundane," Hartzell, now a dentist, recalled. "He came up with the idea of going to see a play in San Francisco. We bought tickets to see Neil Simon's popular Broadway play 'Play It Again, Sam.' John taught me a gentleman etiquette that to this day I still carry out on a daily basis when I am with my wife: That the man is always on the outside when walking down the sidewalk or street. He said, 'This way, if a car veers off the road and onto the sidewalk, the man would be able to act as a shield for the woman.'"

While most of his "wild" behavior was limited to plucking the occasional pomegranate off a neighbor's tree or drenching unsuspecting bicyclists with water balloons launched deftly out of a clever contraption crafted out of his father's surgical supplies, John Riggins was not a prude. He did, like most healthy, well-adjusted Davis boys, and more than a few girls, engage in a rite of passage that was practically obligatory among teens in town.

He went to the Westlane.

Before the legendary Westlane Drive-In adult theater burned in 1986, it provided plenty of hot times. Like an erotic obelisk towering over a patchwork of corn and tomato fields on the sleepy lowland outskirts of South Davis, the Westlane beamed sizzling triple-X pornography on a screen seemingly as big as a football field. No amount of well-intentioned Davis High sex education could prepare the young libido for the sensation of seeing giant genitalia engaged in all kinds of unimaginable acts on this huge screen, partly visible to Interstate 80 motorists and the cause of nervous silence in the front seat and giggles in the back. To a teen boy attending Davis High, where even in the wild late 1970s/early 1980s, the girls were not, compared to other high

1980 newspaper ad for the infamous Westlane Drive-In.

schools in the region, especially known for "putting out," the Westlane was nothing short of manna from sex heaven.

So when some neighborhood boys came back rhapsodizing about their first Westlane visit, John and one of his buddies decided to sneak a peek, with the emphasis on "sneak" — as the only way to see "The Flicks" as a nonpaying, nonadult was to park outside the Westlane's red picket fence, where there was usually competition for the prime parking among overheated teens.

On a warm summer's Wednesday night, the scent of ripening tomatoes and tilled dirt permeating the arid Sacramento Valley air, John and the friend eased along the fence in the friend's family sedan. And, as often happened to first-time teen visitors, the young viewers' wide-eyed triple-X wonder was eclipsed by the flashlight of a Yolo County sheriff's deputy.

"The deputy had this big light shining on us," the friend, one of John's best, recalled with a grin. "We're slinking down, and can't back out. The deputy's got us nose to nose. He gets out of his car, knocks on the window to talk to us, and John's still trying to watch the movie! He takes John's name and address, the whole nine yards."

Let off with a warning, but worried they were in trouble, the boys quickly drove back to John's house, arriving at 10 p.m. John was in a panic.

And sure enough, Dick Riggins was anxiously awaiting their return. *Busted.*

"JOHN...GET INSIDE!" Dick bellowed from the upstairs window as soon as the friend dropped the nervous redhead off. "...'*QUINCY*' IS ON!!," Dick said, referring to the Jack Klugman medical-detective series he and John enjoyed.

And that was the height of John Riggins' mischief. While he had no shortage of rowdy classmates (there was so much drinking his senior year at Davis High that some all-school dances were canceled and one alarmed Davis mother launched what became a national "It's OK Not To Drink" campaign), John Riggins' main outlet for any pent-up energy was the athletic fields of Davis.

Although he was a fleet-footed starting outfielder on the Davis High baseball team, John was best at soccer, a sport the Riggins children grew to love during the family's 1976-1977 sabbatical to Surrey, England, where youngsters played "football" religiously. Although Davis has so many youth soccer leagues now that it's a talent drain on other sports, soccer was something of a fringe sport when John captained the Davis High soccer team. "He was very well-balanced," said John's soccer coach, Eugene "Tash" Tashima, a revered Davis High math teacher for more than 30 years. "Academically, he was a strong student and he brought a lot of that sort of alertness and attention to the team."

Recruited by the Air Force Academy his senior year in high school, he was a top student. "He was the kind of student who handed in an 'A' paper and you handed it back, saying, 'You can do better,'" one of his teachers noted. "He would have made a fine engineer. He liked challenges."

Appearances deceive. John Riggins may have made things look easy in the classroom and on the sporting fields, but it is only because he kept at it. "Unlike the smartest student, the most gifted athlete, John got there by working harder than most of us," said Scott Hill, who knew John since the second grade and is one of about half a dozen guys who considered him his best friend. "Some people are gifted, others are curious; still others break from being plodders to high success by virtue of their own inspiration and sweat. John was far from a plodder, but he took his natural attributes and turned them into high success because he, at an early age, developed a capacity for hard work. He hustled, and showed a tremendous capacity for working."

And lest Davisites and others who knew John Riggins forget the small details that made him so indelible, they will always see that brilliant crimson hair in their mind's eye. Maybe in a dream even, where John Riggins and his fiery red mane are blazing down a soccer field in color, and everything else is in black and white.

That hair. They say it changed with the seasons. Kim Gonsalves, who would likely be John's mother-in-law were he and Sabrina still alive, will, like anybody else who knew John Riggins, never forget it.

"I once was at a park a few years ago," she recalled in 2000. "And a boy about 3 or 4 years old walked by with the same-colored hair as John — and I started crying."

Then she cried again.

"It was *his* hair. I couldn't believe it...John's hair was beautiful. I just loved it."

6
That Smile

"Sabrina would be really pissed to think that she was just a victim.
You don't want to live your whole life and try to be a good person, and
then just be remembered as this murder victim."

— Kim Gonsalves, Sabrina's mother

S abrina Gonsalves was the girl you wanted to babysit your kids, the girl any boy would be proud to bring home to Mom. She was a quiet, responsible person, who, despite being the baby in the family, was the worrier, the peacemaker, the one who made sure the others in the family buckled up before trips.

"She was like a mother hen, yet she was the youngest," Sabrina's father, George, said in a wounded and wistful voice he slips into when talking about his youngest child. "Whenever there were arguments between our other children, she was always there to intervene and try to calm things down."

With her smooth Anglo-Portuguese features, trim, athletic build, candy kiss brown eyes and flowing dark brown hair, Sabrina was a looker. But she was not one who chose to stand out in a crowd: compared to her outgoing older sisters, Sabrina could even be a bit of a wallflower.

All that could change when Sabrina flashed a smile that was both angelic and sexy. Sabrina's smile, not unlike her mother's ear-to-ear mouthful of pearly whites, was beautiful, disarming even. Some names sound elegant and pretty, and Sabrina is one of them. A name Welsh in origin, Celtic legend has it that the name Sabrina derives from a princess who drowned in the Severn, a river in Wales. Kim Gonsalves chose it for her third daughter because she liked the elegant, glamorous Sabrina played by Audrey Hepburn in "Sabrina," a 1954 Billy Wilder fantasy co-starring Humphrey Bogart and William Holden.

Following a labor that was difficult on her mother, Sabrina Gonsalves entered the world in Oakland, Calif., on April 29, 1962, a day on which

**Kim, Andrea and Sabrina Gonsalves
at Andrea's UC Davis graduation.**

Andrea Rosenstein

first lady Jacqueline Kennedy hosted a White House dinner honoring the Nobel Prize Laureates of the Western Hemisphere, Arnold Palmer birdied the 18th hole to win the Texas Open, and the Delta Gamma sorority at Beloit (Wisc.) College was put on probation by its parent organization for "pledging a Negro girl."

Even as a baby she rarely fussed, cried or got into things. "We were worried, she was so calm," her father recalled. "She hardly even sat up. She did whatever we told her to do. Never complained, never hardly ever cried. It was just amazing...we even took her to the doctor to be checked out. They said no, everything seems to be fine."

George Gonsalves, who gave his youngest daughter his Portuguese features, low voice, and quiet, steady nature, met the former Kim Smoot in 1956 at a officer's club swimming pool, where he was relaxing and she was teaching swimming lessons. Neither had had it easy growing up. Kim's parents divorced when she was 9. With a mentally ill mother and a father off fighting the Korean War after remarrying, Kim was essentially on her own on her native Oahu, Hawaii. By age 12 she was babysitting, cooking and cleaning for families that took her in. "I kind of raised myself," said Kim, who is outgoing, outspoken and so nurturing you can't talk to her for five minutes without being offered coffee, a snack, or some variety of maternal concern.

One of six siblings, George hails from a large, hard-working and mostly impoverished and uneducated Portuguese clan that first settled in Hawaii in the 1800s. Laid-back and soft-spoken, he is the son of a mechanic-barber-bookie. The first in his family to attend college, he earned both a bachelor's and master's degree in criminology at San Jose State University, and later a teaching certificate at Columbia University Teachers College in New York.

He has done everything from overseeing a systems management program at USC to selling real estate. But Lt. Col. George Gonsalves, Jr. is first and foremost a military man. A combat veteran of two tours of duty in Vietnam, from where he lovingly wrote his wife daily, George Gonsalves held a variety of jobs in the military, most notably as a language specialist. He has also done extensive counseling of parolees and prisoners, a job that repulsed him after his daughter was murdered.

Despite four children only five years apart in school and a constantly changing menagerie of pets — the family's love of animals is immense — the Gonsalveses moved a lot. Sabrina, for one, lived in more than 21 houses in her 18 years, and seemed to like it. "Moving can be the most exciting thing," Sabrina enthuses with now-sad irony in a 1974 school essay titled "Me, Myself & I." "You think, 'Where I move next may change my life.'"

Every bit as athletic as John Riggins, Sabrina excelled in volleyball, swimming, diving and horseback riding. She paid for her passions: As a young child she broke her arm on a diving board ladder when a boy accidentally pushed her off. On Halloween 1973 she suffered what she endearingly describes in her school essay as "A Painful Incident" — a broken leg sustained when a black feral cat sunk its paws into a hind leg of Sabrina's horse Santana in an Oahu horse stable. In his attempt to shake the cat, Santana kicked Sabrina in the femur, snapping it (and leaving it slightly shorter than the other leg after it healed). Sabrina was flown to Tripler Army Hospital in Honolulu, where, despite being in considerable pain from a body cast during recovery, she wheeled herself on a gurney around the children's ward, reading to kids who were younger or had more serious ailments.

In addition to Hawaii, the family also lived in Kansas; North Carolina; and Heidelberg, Germany, where Sabrina enrolled in high school, beginning in ninth grade. Although there was an English high school for military kids, Sabrina convinced her parents to pay for her to enroll in a private German school so she could learn the language and absorb the culture. "She was discouraged by the headmasters," sister Andrea recalled. "These German students had been together since kindergarten and were not socially forthcoming about Americans. The courses were exclusively in German. Sabrina insisted, and attended school all year. She struggled for months to learn German and break in socially. She was successful and came away with a great appreciation for the culture and language."

The media portrayed Sabrina Gonsalves as shy and retiring. While she, like John, was a bit on the quiet/reserved side ("They were more alike than they were different," Sabrina's mother said), Sabrina was not bashful. She acted in school plays, took it upon herself to be a foreigner with presence at the German school, and looked people squarely in the eye when she talked to them.

She liked frozen yogurt, worried about her weight despite a svelte figure, played the flute, watched "The Sound of Music" so many times on TV with her mom in Germany that her dad started groaning at the sight of it, and preferred soft rock: While John dug the feisty Who and Lynyrd Skynyrd, Sabrina went for the mellower strains of Dan Fogelberg, Fleetwood Mac, Cat Stevens and Boz Skaggs. Together, they settled on a compromise: the Beatles.

And while Sabrina was the model daughter, sister and student — in addition to her athletic prowess and fresh-scrubbed good looks, she got high grades, was an accomplished cook, could knit, adored children and animals, and was a devout Catholic — she did not suffer fools. "She never picked on anybody, she's the youngest, but she was stubborn," her mother said. "When she made up her mind you'd have a hard time changing her mind. The few times I got angry at her when she was a kid, if I (calmly) told her, don't do this, this is making me really upset, she would listen wholeheartedly. But if I got really mad and just marched her into her bedroom, then she would be really mad at me."

Added Andrea: "She would never lose her temper; she would give you the silent treatment for days until you would be so lonely you would find yourself apologizing for anything." Brother Stephen referred to his tenacious little sister as "The Bull."

Sabrina's high morals and stubbornness may very well have cost her her life. "If (whoever killed her) threatened her and she got ticked off at them, they couldn't have moved her for anything," her mother said. "She would not be the type of person who would take any kind of threatening."

When her siblings went off to college in the late 1970s, Sabrina missed them. Beginning in 1977, she spent her summers in Davis, living with Andrea in the family's North Davis condo and working alongside her older sister for the Davis parks department.

George Gonsalves, who in 1980 was an administrator at the Army's Defense Language Institute in Monterey, used a small inheritance to purchase the condo in Covell Commons, a nondescript maze of one- and two-story residences parallel to Covell Boulevard — one of Davis' busiest thoroughfares. While fairly modest, the condo, which is worth close to $400,000 now (the Gonsalveses quickly unloaded it and the bad memories that came with it in the 1980s for about $25,000), is in a great location: Close to shopping, across from Davis' biggest, most functional park, and within bicycling distance of the campus.

Andrea shared the two-bedroom condo with all her siblings at one time or another. When she and Sabrina lived there, they squeezed by on as little as $15 a week on groceries purchased at the Lucky supermarket a half-mile away, where the Gonsalves sisters were regular customers. Oldest sister Terese, meanwhile, eloped in Reno with Carlos Atallah, a Chilean she met while an exchange student in high school, and moved into a small West Davis apartment about a mile away. By 1980, Carlos and Terese had two baby boys.

Sabrina growing up seemed almost oblivious to boys, preferring instead to dream in her teen diary about horses. Despite their considerable good looks, there were no proms, and little interaction with boys for the three Gonsalves sisters in their strict Catholic environment. While dating wasn't forbidden, it was discouraged in favor of school and other activities, which seemed to suit Sabrina just fine.

Until she moved to Davis.

At some point during those first Davis summers while both were still in high school, Sabrina Gonsalves and John Riggins, each employed by the city recreation program for kids, began eyeing each other. During the summer of 1980, while the nation wondered who shot J.R. Ewing in "Dallas," John and Sabrina began wondering about each other in West Davis. John shrewdly made the first move by making sure, whenever possible, the youth teams he coached/mentored at Westwood Park were pitted against Sabrina's teams 2 miles to the east in Redwood Park. Sabrina got the upper hand on at least one occasion: She and co-worker/friend Kim Eichorn and their charges built a winning R2-D2 float for the "Star Wars" Parade and their kids dressed as Sand People. (John's shakily built Starfighter float, on the other hand, fell apart on the way to the parade.) Eichorn recalled Sabrina's nurturing nature in her job as a youth leader at Redwood Park. "Kids really liked her. She was very fun and playful and really got down and played with them. Some rec leaders would just sort of hang out and not really want to do anything with the kids. She was just very good at playing games and leading."

By August 1980, when Sabrina and her protective German shepherd, Shannon, had moved to Davis from Germany for good, John and Sabrina were officially an item, the first real girlfriend for John, the first true beau for Sabrina. They both worked for the city, were enrolled that fall at UC Davis, even had a couple of classes together, including a tough freshmen English class that threw both John and Sabrina for a loop, a humbling bit of college comeuppance. "John and Sabrina had never really seen a very low grade in their lives," John's mother, Kate, said, grinning. "And in freshmen English, they saw many red lines on their papers."

From August 1980 until the night they disappeared in the macabre December fog, John and Sabrina were inseparable to the point that they insisted on holding hands while pedaling their bicycles side by side on the flat streets of Davis. While they were so smitten with each other that their mothers shared concerns about the whirlwind suddenness of the relationship, John and Sabrina never slept together during their five months as a couple. Despite the pre-AIDS promiscuity of the times, the sweethearts had, by all appearances, an old-fashioned courtship. "Sabrina was a virgin," Andrea volunteered. "And they just did not (have sex). But I think that they snuggled and kissed."

John and Sabrina did indeed dream of a life together. And to Sabrina, who idolized oldest sister Terese, happily married with two kids by her early 20s, such dreams seemed entirely natural. "Sabrina told me everything," Andrea noted. "John wanted to get a double degree; he was going to get an engineering degree and a bioscience degree. Then, with a master's in engineering he was going to go to medical school, because he wanted to do biomedical engineering and invent things. He was interested in limbs. They had it all figured out. They were going to get married after two years."

Sabrina, Andrea added, planned to transfer to Sacramento State to get a nursing degree. Then she was going to work and help put John through school. "She was going to have children before he totally finished his residency. Terese and Carlos had kids while in college, so they saw it as a real possibility. And they wanted to have six kids, and they had names for them."

Sabrina's family met John twice in 1980, first in September, when the couple stopped in Monterey on the way to a camping trip to Yosemite, during which Sabrina had to be treated in the emergency room for a bee sting and John stumbled upon some of his UC Davis soccer teammates — and promptly ran away for fear of being teased for being seen with his new girl.

John and Sabrina in Monterey, November 1980.

Andrea Rosenstein

"We walked around the Monterey wharf and up through the woods behind their house," John wrote in a letter to a high school friend following the visit to the Gonsalves home. "They live in military quarters that are really nice — not barracks. It's pretty funny seeing everyone walk around in uniforms saluting everyone else."

John and Sabrina visited Monterey again on Thanksgiving 1980. It's a wonderful memory for the Gonsalves family, as magical as Christmas a month later was horrible. The Friday after that Thanksgiving was spent frolicking on the beach in Carmel, playing football, having fun with Terese's baby boys. That Friday is the last time Kim Gonsalves had her entire family together, an occasion she commemorates by wearing a bracelet her husband gave her, simply inscribed: *Thanksgiving 1980.*

Just before John and Sabrina climbed in the Rigginses' little blue Honda Civic full of Thanksgiving leftovers Kim had packed them that Friday, Sabrina's mother French-braided her hair while urging Sabrina and John to hit the road back to Davis as it was 5 p.m. and getting late.

"Mom," a radiant Sabrina purred as Kim lovingly arranged her youngest child's silky tresses in crisscross patterns from behind. "There's so much I want to tell you about John. I'm just dying to talk to you, but it's going to have to wait.

"When I come back at Christmas I just have to tell you all kinds of things about John."

Joel Davis

That Smile

7
November

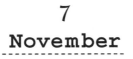

Mary Beth Sowers and Craig Miller, attractive, athletic and bright sweethearts attending Sacramento State University, were living large on Saturday night, Nov. 2, 1980. The young couple, engaged to be married, had spent a dreamy night socializing with about 120 friends and gliding across the dance floor at a Founder's Day Dance. Miller's fraternity, Delta Sigma Chi, put on the gala in the downstairs banquet room of the Carousel restaurant in Arden Fair Mall, then the most popular shopping center in Sacramento.

The dark-haired Miller, 22, dressed in slacks and sport jacket, and Sowers, 21, a blonde beauty in an ice-blue, floor-length dress, left the party just after 1 a.m., emerging from the Carousel's cozy warmth to the cold, damp, expansive mall parking lot.

Andy Beal, 22, a strapping 6-foot 5-inch fraternity brother of Miller's, left the party minutes later. Beal noticed Miller and Sowers sitting quietly in the back seat of a silver and blue two-door Olds Cutlass.

Perhaps a little buzzed from the white Russians he had drunk, a playful Beal thought he'd do some practical joking. Noticing an open driver's door, he jumped in the car. In the front passenger seat sat a stocky man with a hawkish face – Gerald Armand Gallego, 34. Gallego and his wife, Charlene, had kidnapped the sweethearts at random just minutes earlier. Gerald wanted a sex slave. With her beauty queen looks, Sowers was just right. When Beal squeezed into the car, Gallego coolly concealed the gun. "Get out of here," Miller said calmly to Beal as Miller sat still on the blue crushed velour back seat, perhaps saving Beal's life while further risking his own. "This is no place for you. Get out of here."

Beal climbed out of the car. Charlene got in his face. A pretty, petite blonde who, despite being seven months pregnant by Gerald, was still rail thin, Charlene brazenly slapped the fraternity boy twice her size in the face. "What the fuck are you doing in my car?" she hissed.

Charlene had angrily stormed out of the car in a futile effort to fetch some

Mary Beth Sowers

car keys Miller had tossed out the back seat window in a desperate move to attract attention. She then got back behind the wheel. While a drunk, gloating and sex-crazed Gerald Gallego held a .25 caliber handgun on the terrified couple, she peeled out of the parking lot.

Beal, stunned and angry, his cheek red from Charlene's hand, memorized the car's license plate — 240 ROV — as it exited Arden Fair and headed for the freeway. As Charlene drove to a remote spot in the foothills, Gerald Gallego robbed Miller of $20 and ordered him to remove his shoes. When Charlene found a suitably rural spot, Bass Lake Road in the El Dorado Hills area east of Sacramento, Gallego ordered Miller out of the car at gunpoint. Illuminated by the headlights, with Charlene and a terrified Sowers looking on, Gallego shot Miller once in the back of the head.

Miller crumbled on the wet grass. Gallego then unloaded two more rounds into the young man's skull to make sure he was dead. In all, Miller had been shot once above the right ear, once at the right cheekbone, and once in the neck.

Gallego then had Charlene drive back to his dumpy Sacramento apartment, where he marched Sowers into the bedroom at gunpoint. While Charlene slept and watched TV in the front room, Gallego repeatedly raped the young beauty, who pleaded and cried for him to stop.

Just before sunrise, Gallego emerged from the bedroom with a stunned Sowers. He then had Charlene drive them back to the foothills. This time they stopped on a desolate spot off Sierra College Boulevard, a long, rural road that winds past Sierra College in Placer County.

As he had done with Miller, Gallego led a stumbling Mary Beth, her hands bound with the ribbon from her blue dress, from the car, and emptied three rounds into her head — *pop, pop, pop.* A promising life that had developed over 21 years ended in seconds behind a small hill in the middle of nowhere. Mary Beth Sowers' body would not be found for 20 days.

Meanwhile, Andy Beal worried about his friends. He decided not to call the police following a meeting with two fraternity brothers in the parking lot after Miller and Sowers left in the strangers' Oldsmobile. But he fretted enough to return to the mall parking lot at 6 a.m.

Beal noted Mary Beth Sowers' red Honda Civic still parked there. The keys Miller tossed in desperation hours before were beneath the car, the doors unlocked, Sowers' expensive coat on the front seat. Beal flagged down a police patrolman and reported the odd occurrence.

Knowing Beal had seen them, the Gallegos tried to cover their tracks that Sunday morning. They tossed Sowers' purse and other incriminating evidence into the Sacramento River, Miller's shoes in a Dumpster. They hastily purchased a blanket to cover Miller's body, but when they returned to the site where Gerald Gallego killed him, the body had been discovered, removed, and the area sealed by authorities. Panic set in.

Police traced the Olds license plate, finding the car registered to Charlene's doting father, a wealthy Sacramento supermarket executive who lived in upscale Arden Park. The authorities were told who had the car. By the time Charlene and Gerald drove back to Gerald's apartment, it swarmed with police.

The couple then fled to Reno, where, having seen headlines about the murders of two popular college kids, they dumped the Olds, and then hopped on a Greyhound bus to Salt Lake City. After stopping in Colorado, where they conned their way into getting enough information for birth certificates and assumed names, they made their way to Omaha, Neb. Charlene's parents knew their daughter was on the run with Gallego, but did not know exactly why, though they knew Gallego was bad news.

On Monday, Nov. 4, Gallego's half-brother, David Hunt, called Charlene's mother, Mercedes. Hunt sounded so much like Gallego, at first she thought it was him.

"Mrs. Williams, this is David Hunt. I know you don't like my family, but is there anything I can do to help Charlene or Gerry?"

Mercedes Williams didn't take long to reply.

"They do not need yours or anybody else's help. Goodbye."

The Williamses wired their daughter money in Salt Lake City, but they decided to alert the FBI when Charlene asked for more money to be sent to Omaha. The Gallegos were arrested at 11:30 in the morning on Nov. 17 as Charlene attempted to retrieve money through her parents at an Omaha Western Union office.

Including the Miller and Sowers murders, which were sloppy and involved the type of beloved, well-to-do victims that attract considerable of media and police attention, authorities would eventually link Gerald Gallego to 10 sex-slave killings. Nine of his victims were female, one of them pregnant. While it was the sex-slave slayings, Sacramento County's dogged detective work, and damning testimony by Charlene that would put him on death row, Gallego was a lifelong criminal who got started early. He and David Hunt, for instance, were arrested for burglary as far back as 1958 in their hometown of Sacramento.

David Hunt had been committing crimes for 20 years when he violated his probation by stealing sheets from a San Jose Holiday Inn in 1978. After serving time, Hunt was paroled from San Quentin Prison on Oct. 10, 1980. It didn't take long for Hunt to get back into trouble. Six days after Gallego was arrested under the alias Stephen Feil, Hunt engineered a daring prison escape of his former San Quentin cellblock neighbor Richard Thompson. The breakout had the trappings of a B-movie.

The muscular Hunt and the slight, balding Thompson were no strangers to prison escapes. After being arrested for a botched robbery in Vallejo in 1969, Hunt and Gallego escaped from the Solano County Jail by sawing through the window bars of their third-floor cell. They were captured in San Francisco several days later, but not before a Solano County hotel robbery during which Hunt squeezed the trigger on a .45 caliber handgun at a sheriff's deputy who interrupted the crime. The gun didn't go off, police said, because its clip was not in all the way.

Thompson, on the other hand, escaped from prison in Chino, Calif., in 1975 after being sent there for robbery. He was captured a day later, but not before exchanging gunfire with authorities. On Nov. 24, 1980, the two "road dogs," as they liked to call each other, were at it again. Thompson, in San Quentin for violating his parole by stealing a car, had a 9 a.m. medical appointment for a hearing problem in nearby Greenbrae. Following the exam, a prison guard began escorting the manacled Thompson out of the medical office.

"Wait, I need to blow my nose," Thompson said coolly, trying to buy some time as he was walked back to the doctor's office for a Kleenex. After the purposeful delay, the guard again led Thompson from the facility.

On a bench in the lobby sat David Hunt, his head down, his flinty black eyes locked on the floor. His face darkened by charcoal, Hunt wore a wig and was armed with a shotgun. Authorities said the wig and shotgun were provided to Hunt by his girlfriend, Suellen, a former San Quentin intake counselor with whom he was living at Suellen's Menlo Park home.

As a San Quentin guard and medical assistant popped open the transport van's rear door, Thompson, despite being handcuffed to belly chains, managed to snatch the keys. The bizarrely disguised Hunt appeared and ordered the pair into the back of the van. "Be quiet, keep your eyes down and you won't get hurt," he yelled. Thompson managed to get into the driver's side seat and started the van while Hunt jumped into the front passenger's seat.

"I've got tape," Hunt said to Thompson, suggesting that they use it to restrain the pair in the back.

"No time for that," Thompson shot back.

They then tore out the van's two-way radio from the dash, and snatched the San Quentin guard's whistle. "Stay here and stay quiet for five minutes," they warned. "If not, we have a friend nearby who will blow you away."

Thompson and Hunt locked the pair inside the van and fled to a getaway car driven by Thompson's wife, Valerie, who helped plan the escape. The trio then embarked on a crime spree through six Western states, robbing stores and gas stations when they needed cash.

Hunt's wig and Thompson's San Quentin belly and leg chains were found Nov. 30 — six days after the San Quentin escape — dangling from a tree in Kelso, Wash.

8
Lost...

Most Davis residents at the time remember where they were when word
trickled out during the ominous weekend when fall officially disappeared into winter, Sabrina and John mysteriously disappeared in the tule
fog and Davis the way locals knew it simply disappeared.

I was in Leo Edson's Ford Comet. In addition to driving this ugly burnt-
yellow car so recklessly around corners that my dad once chewed him out,
Leo liked to argue. So did I. The 49ers, Giants, girls, teachers, bands (real
battles here), more girls, top barber downtown, best beer. Guy talk.

So it was a rare truce in the Comet debates when Leo turned to me casu-
ally during a Christmas shopping outing in Davis on the morning of Dec.
22, 1980, as I routinely tamped a pinch of Copenhagen snuff into my lower
lip and he rounded a corner too fast:

"Did you hear about Riggins?"

"No" (*spit*). "Redheaded John Riggins who graduated last year?"

"Yeah ... Riggins is missing."

Riggins is Missing. For a day and a half, the worried refrain jolted the holiday happiness of Davis.

My 18th birthday was three days prior, Dec. 19, 1980. I do not remember
a thing about it. It is eclipsed by *Riggins is Missing*. Like a frantic version of
the children's game post office, word spread fast in Davis: the All-American
Boy in the All-American Town cannot be found. What to do?

Sabrina was missing, too. But she was not a local, few knew of her. Not
much in the way of Sabrina is Missing percolating on the streets of Davis.
But Sabrina's two older sisters knew right away on Sunday morning that
something was wrong.

When Andrea awoke that interminable day, she again heard the hollow
whir of the bathroom fan she left on the night before. "As soon as I heard the
fan, I knew Sabrina never came home," Andrea recalled. "She would have
turned the fan off."

Andrea dragged her flu-weakened body out of bed and peeked into her younger sister's room. No Sabrina. But Sabrina's wallet was in plain view, her bed still made. Her clothes and belongings were laid out neatly for a trip that day down to the family's Monterey home for the holidays. Sabrina's suitcase sat packed next to some presents she had carefully wrapped.

Sabrina's father, George, an Army-trained early riser, by now was on his way from Monterey to fetch his daughters, only to learn during a stop at his mother's home in Hayward that his youngest could not be found. When Sabrina's mom, Kim, learned her daughter was missing, she rushed out to a Catholic church in Monterey and prayed for her.

The surprise party the night before started about 7 and ended around 10. At first there was anger. Anger that Sabrina and John could be so unusually callous as to blow off the birthday, probably in favor of a Beatles tribute at Cinema 2 in the wake of John Lennon's recent assassination. (This is what they told Andrea they would be doing so as not to tip off her surprise party.) Confusion added to the anger. Because it was a surprise party, Sabrina and John had been coy with Andrea about their plans that night. "They made elaborate plans for that day and into the evening to throw me off," Andrea recalled. "We all assumed they had to work until too late, so they continued on to see the late movie."

Saturday night's ire became serious concern at first light on Sunday morning. The concern turned to outright dread as the day wore on. About 7:30 a.m., a hysterical Andrea called Terese. The sisters then exchanged harried phone calls with John's parents.

Kate and Dick Riggins had just gotten used to sleeping soundly when their oldest child was out at night. After all, he was now 18 with a girlfriend and a life of his own. So they dozed off comfortably Saturday night even though John had not come in. They were up early Sunday because Dick was scheduled to read the Holy Eucharist Rite Two at the 9:15 a.m. service at Episcopal Church of St. Martin.

After the Gonsalves girls called, John's parents peeked into his room. Farrah Fawcett smiled teasingly from the wall, but John was not in the bed, which was still made. They checked outside. No sign of the bulky two-tone family van John borrowed the night before in the driveway or along the shiny-wet asphalt of narrow Bucknell Drive. John clearly had not come home. And despite a new girlfriend, this was downright un-John-like.

While John's sister, Carrie, 16, pedaled her bike to tell the church elders her dad would have to cancel reading the lesson, Kate and Dick worked the phones, calling friends, area hospitals, anyone or anything that would have information. Other than verifying that, yes, the young sweethearts definitely had been seen working the city parks department's bustling, 135-child production of "The Nutcracker" the night before, not much was known.

Both families immediately ruled out irresponsible behavior. Eloping, staying out all night partying, a spur-of-the-moment trip somewhere were not considered. Too out of character. Foul play? Possibly, *but this was Davis.*

Given the weather — forecasts called it "dreary and drippy" — it had to be a car accident.

Friends were contacted. The fog had subsided; now there was misty, intermittent rain. The soggy, glistening back roads of rural outer Davis were combed. Mostly the tricky, accident-prone roads running west of Davis to Winters and north to Woodland. Nobody thought to look east to Sacramento because those roads were well-traveled. Surely a wreck would be seen there.

With the searches futile, the families decided to press the police and the media. Although the Sacramento TV stations had skeletal crews on Sundays, Dick Riggins got lucky when he pounded on the door of KXTV Channel 10. The employee who answered turned out to be one of Riggins' patients, who in turn used his influence to get a report on the late Sunday night news. Like a bad cliché, the 11 p.m. news that Sunday opened with snapshots of the missing couple and the van, while the anchorman intoned, "Authorities in Davis fear the worst ..."

Initially, Davis police maintained the kids had not been gone long enough to be considered missing persons. John and Sabrina would have to have been missing until 8 the following morning — 24 hours after they were reported unaccounted for — to be officially considered missing. "They probably went to Reno to elope or something," the families were told. "Happens all the time."

Although Terese, the oldest Gonsalves girl, did in fact get married in Reno, the families dug in their heels. No way. Not these two. So Rigginses and Gonsalveses descended on the Davis Police Department's quaint mission-style building in the middle of the quaint town. They demanded to talk to the watch commander.

Even while her son was missing, Kate Riggins maintained her Southern protocol, passing out coffee to the officers while Andrea Gonsalves got in their faces and her father stood by quietly in support.

"Look, you cannot convince me they ran away," Andrea said. "Sabrina never goes anywhere without her toothbrush. She doesn't have her ID, she doesn't have her wallet, she doesn't have any clothes; she packed nothing. These are not impulsive kids."

The Davis Police Department has had its flaws over the years (one joke I heard as a young reporter at a time when there were many unsolved homicides: If you want to get away with murder do it in Davis), but lack of compassion is generally not one of them. If relatives of missing local kids come in pleading for help, one of them a sister who does not take no for an answer, they won't be told to take a number.

About 7:20 p.m. that Sunday a young on-duty Davis officer, Fred Turner, whose career, reputation and life would be forever tied to John and Sabrina, began alerting other law-enforcement agencies that the pair were missing. At 11 p.m. family members had a brainstorming session with a Davis police detective. By now they had convinced the police foul play was likely. At 12:07 a.m. Monday, Dec. 22, while most of Davis slept, the case was reclassified as a kidnapping.

West Coast law-enforcement agencies and the FBI were told to be on the lookout for the girl with the smile and the boy with the red hair.

9
...Found

"... And then the foolishness of the body will be cleared away and we
shall be pure and hold converse with other pure souls, and know of
ourselves the clear light everywhere; and this is surely the light of truth.
For no impure thing is allowed to approach the pure."

— Plato ("The Phaedo")

The 1972 rerouting of U.S. Highway 50 through Sacramento rendered adjacent Folsom Boulevard — Sacramento's once-mighty thoroughfare — into a funky patchwork of second-tier, 1950s-era bars and restaurants, aging motels, trailer parks and businesses attracted to cheap leases.

To this day, much of Folsom Boulevard remains a low-brow mishmash that has seen better days, but a road that still holds a certain seedy allure, like a tired midway on a seaside boardwalk. At the east end of Folsom Boulevard, where the flat Sacramento terrain starts bowing to the El Dorado foothills, on the steely gray morning of Dec. 22, 1980, sat an ominous new attraction: the Riggins family van.

The tan and white 1977 Chevrolet van that John and Sabrina filled with birthday presents, ice cream and youthful exuberance befitting the van's red "Milk's A Kick!" bumper sticker early on Saturday night, was discovered at 8 a.m. Monday by a Folsom Police patrolman following a report of a "suspicious van" near Aerojet. It was in plain view under a tree about 30 feet off the road and near Hazel Avenue, a short walk from Rudy's Hideaway bar and supper club. The doors were locked, the keys tucked under the driver's side floor mat. The tires were muddy.

The van was in plain sight. John and Sabrina were not.

Folsom police radioed Davis police and the Sacramento County Sheriff's Department that the van had been found. At 9:25 a.m. the van was towed to the Sacramento County Crime Lab for fingerprinting and an evidence check.

The Riggins van found abandoned Dec. 22, 1980.

At 10:35 a.m. the van was moved to the county storage facility to be photographed. Police, sheriff's deputies and reporters descended on the area.

About 11 a.m., Davis police Detective Gene Burton and a Folsom officer walked north from where the van had been to a rural area between Folsom Boulevard and Highway 50. They noticed a small dirt road with recent tire tracks. They followed the muddy road into a wooded area, where there was a small ravine, about 7 feet deep.

It was here in the cold December mist with oblivious motorists whooshing past on the highway below that Burton discovered the stiff, soggy bodies of two well-dressed young adults. Closer to the top of the ravine lay a male body face up in a brown sweater, brown shirt, tan slacks and tan leather shoes.

About 12 feet away and closer to the bottom lay a female body face down in a black velour jacket, white blouse, a plaid skirt pulled up to her buttocks, and black boots, her bare knees scraped from being tossed.

Rigor mortis had set in. The faces of both bodies and all limbs save the young woman's legs were tightly wrapped in silver duct tape; clear filament packing tape was used on both sets of wrists. The tape was cut on both victims' wrists and the male's legs, apparently to make it easier to toss them in the ravine like so much garbage.

The positive identification would not come until Riggins family friend and onetime Davis Mayor Jerry Adler drove to Sacramento with Dr. Riggins and viewed the bodies at the Sacramento County morgue about 1 p.m. It was John and Sabrina, something the authorities had known for hours.

The autopsies, John's performed at 3:30 p.m. by one pathologist, Sabrina's at 4 p.m. by another, showed the sweethearts died equally awful deaths for opposite reasons.

John had been beaten with five blows to the head, and his throat cut, but the knife avoided major arteries. It likely took hours to die in that soggy ravine. He perhaps could have been saved by passersby, including a sheriff's patrolman who noticed the van at 2 a.m. the night of the kidnapping but did not know the vehicle was part of a crime.

Sabrina, by contrast, suffered two deep, savage cuts that severed her jugular, and she died instantly. She was nearly decapitated. Authorities at the time did not think she had been sexually assaulted.

The Davis Enterprise is a small afternoon daily that around Christmastime normally features warm holiday stories and wire copy filler on Page 1. The bodies were found right before the presses rolled that Monday. But they had yet to be officially identified. Frustrated editors therefore settled on a compromise, running high school yearbook photos of John and Sabrina under a we-can't-say-but-you-figure-it-out banner headline:

UC DAVIS STUDENTS MISSING
BODIES FOUND NEAR VAN; NOT IDENTIFIED

But everyone knew.

Just like that, the Riggins family lost its oldest child, taken on his parents' wedding anniversary. The Gonsalves family lost its youngest, found dead on her sister/best friend/roommate's 22nd birthday.

Davis lost its innocence.

Joel Davis

...Pound

10
Goodbye

----

*"How could anyone be abducted in our town? Those sorts of things
don't happen to good people in a nice little town."*

— Kim Eichorn, Friend of John and Sabrina

Within days of her oldest child being found brutally murdered in a soggy
ravine off a freeway, Kate Riggins — not one to express emotion in public — didn't cry, didn't faint, didn't panic.

Instead, she went shopping.

Despite a shock that practically brought Davis to its knees, despite a
sense of terror that gripped the community, the Ragginses' first priority was
maintaining a sense of normalcy for their surviving children, Robert and
Carrie, a protective streak that continues to this day. They decided that the
best thing to do in the wake of John and Sabrina's deaths was to go ahead
with a planned Christmas vacation skiing trip the very next week to Kirkwood Mountain Resort, which treated the family to skiing in exchange for
Dr. Riggins being on call.

The family needed groceries for the trip, and Kate, who had just dealt with
her own father's death a month prior to John's ("it was almost like a rehearsal")
went to Safeway at University Mall to get them herself. In the checkout line,
a bag boy recognized the redhead with the Tennessean accent as a regular.
The smiling lad offered his obligatory "And how are you today, ma'am?"

"I'm not very good," Kate replied calmly. "My son has just been murdered."

People have a range of emotions when grieving. Kate's response, and her
family's in general, was not to show it outside the home. Oh, there was weeping: Robert cried in the shower, his tears blending with the hot needles of
water cascading off his shoulders. Carrie and her father shared tears quietly
together in the family's normally happy living room, a sad contrast to the
brightly painted walls and the cheerful carousel horse.

The two families reacted in character. While the Ragginses mostly held it together with WASP reserve, the Gonsalveses, the more emotionally open of the two clans, were more demonstrative in their grief: Upon hearing from a Riggins family friend that her daughter was found murdered, Kim Gonsalves dropped the phone and fainted in her Monterey home. Her son, Stephen, was there to revive her. Just a year older than Sabrina and extremely close to her, Stephen soon lost it, pounding his fists on the carpet.

Sabrina's lanky and soft-spoken father, George, who'd seen his share of tragedy in Vietnam and in his job counseling criminals, feared the worst from the moment he arrived in Davis the day before the bodies were found. Even before John and Sabrina were discovered dead, he methodically directed Sabrina's two older sisters to drive home to their mother in Monterey that fateful Monday. In measured tones, he broke the news to Andrea — on her 22nd birthday — at a pay phone outside a McDonald's in San Jose. "They ... found ... their ... bodies ..."

It would be years before George Gonsalves could go back to rehabilitating criminals. He simply couldn't face thieves, rapists, con men and murderers, let alone help them.

The contrasts didn't end in how the families grieved. The Rigginses, well-known in Davis, were in a fish bowl, nearly overwhelmed with well-meaning attention and concern. It also made for some awkwardness when the family ventured out in public: When Carrie and Robert returned to school in January, they were now each the Murdered Boy's Sibling.

And while Kate stayed in control of herself while in the awkward situation, the awkward situation was often out of her control. A lot of people simply did not know what to say or do. "I had many people who moved to another aisle of the supermarket when they saw me," she said. "And then others who just broke down and cried in the middle of the store. The whole gamut."

The Gonsalveses experienced the same awkwardness. "We lost friends because of this. Lifetime friends who couldn't handle it," George Gonsalves noted. "They didn't want to talk about it, so we just sort of lost contact."

The Gonsalveses, who in their nomadic military world rarely lived in one place for long, grieved in near-anonymous isolation at their new Monterey home. "Nobody came to answer our phone, nobody came to help us in Monterey," Kim said, shaking her head. "We didn't have any neighbors or friends to help us. It was really hard."

But even such anonymity couldn't shield the family from fresh reminders of a case that made national headlines. Both families were inundated by the media. Both say they were, for the most part, treated respectfully, with one lingering exception that incites anger and anguish to this day: Pictures of the sweethearts' corpses being taken from the ditch in body bags, a gruesome image that ran on TV and in many newspapers.

"We had just found out (the bodies were found), and the children had turned on the TV at 11 at night," Kim Gonsalves recalled angrily. "We're all crying and sitting around and we are all devastated. All of sudden we look up and there's Sabrina being carried away in a body bag with her boots sticking out. The boots I bought her in Italy! Handmade leather boots! It just devastated me."

The media also showed a sympathetic side, at least in Davis. The Davis Enterprise summed up the community's shock and sadness in its annual holiday editorial, which ran under a headline reading, "Season A Little Empty; But Christmas Hope Alive." "It is normally a very festive time of year," the editorial noted. "But in our community this Christmas season, we are a little empty. The murders of John Riggins and Sabrina Gonsalves leave us with a hollow feeling."

Hollow. Stunned. And very, very afraid. Suddenly, in a city so secure it was mocked for its over-regulation, children weren't allowed out of view, teenagers were given tighter curfews. Walking the dog on a dark bike path behind my home, normally a relaxing pastime, suddenly felt creepy.

Davis had been flattened by a sucker punch from out of the fog and didn't know where it came from.

"How could anyone be abducted in our town?" said Kim Eichorn, who knew both John and Sabrina well. "Those sorts of things don't happen to good people in a nice little town. I think it burst that whole bubble of fantasy of the way life was and the way it would be."

The memorial was midmorning the day after Christmas — another dismal, foggy December Davis day — at Episcopal Church of St. Martin, the Riggins family church, a church set off by its odd post-modern architecture, namely a strangely shaped, wood-shingled roof. Just days before *Time* magazine would name President-Elect Ronald Reagan its Man of the Year while Jimmy Carter nursed a broken collarbone from a ski accident, some 500 mourners packed the church to say goodbye to John and Sabrina. Another 300 huddled outside in the damp cold to hear the nondenominational service on loudspeakers. This despite UC Davis being on Christmas break and the town fairly empty.

Hugs were tight, tears loose. The prim and proper church organist, who never played anything besides hymnals, made an exception on this day, performing John and Sabrina's favorite Beatles songs, "Yesterday" and "Let it Be," made all the more melancholy by John Lennon's murder 17 days before.

"We wonder how it can happen to two beautiful people," the Rev. Bill Burrill, a Riggins family friend, told the throngs of devastated mourners. "Don't be afraid to scream out 'damn.' We can keep saying 'why, why, why,' and we can wonder how dark the world will be."

The memorial proved a necessary healing for a reeling community, if not for the families, who were on display, including being filmed leaving the church by newspaper photographers and TV crews. Undercover detectives eyed the mourners, looking for possible suspects or leads in the baffling case. Even family members were eyed with suspicion. "The memorial was huge and overwhelming and felt like it was some kind of social event," Carrie Riggins said.

The families said goodbye more privately. John was cremated, his ashes scattered in Yosemite early in 1981, where he and Sabrina happily visited just two months before they died. John's immediate family took turns scattering his ashes. And being out of public view, tears flowed freely this time.

In addition to the Davis service, the military held a memorial for Sabrina on Dec. 24 in Monterey at the Monterey Presidio. Her body was eventually flown to Hawaii, where her parents had her buried alongside relatives at National Memorial Cemetery of the Pacific (aka "Punchbowl") in Honolulu.

Found in Sabrina's right hand before her body was prepared for burial were two strands of John Riggins' red hair.

11
Why?

Following the murder of her sister, roommate and confidante, Andrea Gonsalves showed amazing control of herself. Not only did she have to deal with the devastating loss of Sabrina, but because other family members were overcome with grief or too far away, Andrea bore the brunt of picking up the pieces. This included everything from closing Sabrina's bank account to dealing with the police investigators to arranging the memorial to speaking with the media to working with crime-prevention groups.

On top of that, Andrea came home every night to the North Davis condo she had shared with her murdered sister, a condo that was, chillingly enough, the possible abduction site. She could not walk two feet without being reminded of Sabrina. "Every night I'm not eating because I go home to my house at night and dinner is just devastating," she said. She also had a hard time finding a roommate. "Nobody else would move in with me after Sabrina died. Who wants to live with someone whose sister was kidnapped and murdered?"

It was ordinary life that kept the victims' families sane after the tragedy, and Andrea tried her best to lead one. A graduate student in psychology who taught classes at UC Davis on her way to a master's, Andrea decided not long after the murders that it might be therapeutic to get back to studying. She headed to the bustling UC Davis Coffeehouse – comforting, warm and never lacking for human interaction – to hit the books. Nursing a bagel and a coffee at a little round table, Andrea couldn't help but overhear two coeds discussing the murders.

"Did you hear about the students who were murdered over Christmas?" one girl gossiped to the other. "Oh yeah, I read about that. You know they must have been doing drugs. It probably was a drug deal gone sour."

Andrea felt sick to her stomach.

"I thought I was going to die," she said. "I cannot tell you how upset I was. To think that the world out there was thinking that about my sister. And I couldn't speak to these people, couldn't open my mouth to tell them how horrified I was. I just grabbed all my stuff and I ran."

A drug deal gone sour. A scorned lover. A money squabble. In a world of human failings, people automatically assumed whoever killed John and Sabrina had a motive having to do with ... John and Sabrina. Given that many mistook the Gonsalves Portuguese surname as Hispanic in a town where the worst is often assumed about crimes involving Hispanic names, given that two other college sweethearts had already been murdered in Davis in March, given that love is transitory and fragile in college towns, a love-triangle theory seemed especially popular, in part because some wrongly interpreted that the Riggins van's personalized license, "3S MUM," had a group-sex connotation. (The vanity plate was inspired by Kate Riggins' nickname of "Three's Mum" when her family lived in England.)

But the truth is John and Sabrina were so good, so unsoiled by the temptations and vices of young adulthood, that their squeaky-clean pasts actually hurt the investigation of their case.

"There just wasn't anything," said Sacramento County homicide detective Stan Reed, who has worked on some 400 homicides in his career, including as the initial lead detective in the Riggins-Gonsalves case. A stocky, fair-skinned man with an expressive face (the actor Ned Beatty comes to mind), Reed is an old-school gumshoe who likes to beat his palms on his desk for emphasis when making points.

There just (*thump...*) wasn't (*thump...*) anything (*THUMP-THUMP!*).

Murder detectives know that the first 48 hours after a killing are crucial to solving it. The killer or killers are more vulnerable psychologically, more apt to be unnerved by a detective — even a detective who has little more to go on than a bluff and a scare — asking probing questions. The killers are also less likely to have disposed of all damning evidence.

In this case, John and Sabrina lay in that ditch parallel to Highway 50 for up to 40 hours before they were found dead, giving the killer(s) a head start on avoiding detection.

"If you can get to somebody quick enough, their psychological defenses are down," explained Lt. Ray Biondi, the head of the Sacramento County homicide unit at the time of the murders and something of a legend in Sacramento law enforcement, in part because of his work in bringing Gerald Gallego to justice. "They just killed somebody, and four hours later there's a homicide detective knocking on the door. And they often think we know

Lt. Ray Biondi
Sacramento Bee

a hell of a lot more than we really know. A lot of cases are solved that easily: We ask the person to go downtown and start interviewing. Whether they lie or not doesn't make much difference. If they are truly the people responsible, if they do all their denials, they are likely just to bury themselves."

Unfortunately, there was nobody to bring downtown in this case, though a killer of two college sweethearts six weeks earlier in Sacramento —Gallego — was there. In jail.

Although finding the bulky Riggins van parked in plain sight under a tree on a wet gravel shoulder off Folsom Boulevard suggested to some detectives the murders were being "advertised," there was little evidence. The bushy ditch where the bodies were found was a dreary cesspool for the vices of humanity: not far from a rundown trailer park, it was used for everything from discarded furniture to target practice to a drinking spot. Collected for possible evidence in the general area of the bodies were several empty alcohol containers, some shotgun shell casings (of little help since a knife or razor was the murder weapon), and a boot. A little blood from both victims' heads was collected off some grass. It rained the day before the bodies were found; some blood washed away.

The van yielded more clues, but not many — at least not in this time of pre-DNA forensics. A black tire iron was found out of its holder on the floor in the back of the van. John Riggins likely tried to fight off his abductor(s), which would be in character given how protective he was toward Sabrina. Found with deep bruises on his skull and scratches on his arms, John was beaten to the point of unconsciousness by a blunt object. The tire iron made sense.

Homicide detectives like to withhold certain details from the public so they can trip up any possible suspects down the line. John's beating and the extensive use of duct and clear filament tape binding both victims were the key details kept secret in this case, but word soon got out. The San Francisco Chronicle, for one, within a week of the killings reported that the victims might have been restrained with tape. And John's beating was a fast rumor around Davis: I learned about it from a police-friendly Davis High School basketball coach on a team bus ride home from a game, where discussion of the murders was a hotter topic than the game itself.

Dr. Anthony Cunha, the pathologist who did Sabrina's autopsy, reported that Sabrina had not been sexually assaulted. He later testified to this in court:

Q: "There was no sign of sexual molestation of her?"

A: "None."

But there were some ominous signs that had some investigators wondering otherwise from the get-go.

For starters, unlike John, Sabrina's legs were not bound, suggesting access to her lower body was sought. She had a bruise on her vagina, though that could have come from possibly being kicked into the ravine. Sabrina was found face down on her knees, her knuckles dirty, possibly suggesting she was made to get on all fours when assaulted.

Sabrina's white, size 4 Maidenform bikini panties were also inside out and twisted, perhaps suggesting someone shoved them back on her incorrectly in haste after an assault. But Sabrina had boots on, over which the panties — or both the boots and panties — would have had to be removed and put back on, an awkward, time-consuming process given that the killer(s) seemed to be in a hurry. (One foot was partially out of one of the boots.) Plus, why would a killer go to so much trouble to redress Sabrina, only to toss her into a ditch?

Finally, the panties were a plain white bikini style, a type that looks similar inside or out.

"If it was dark and she was in a hurry, Sabrina could have put them on inside out," noted Andrea, who, amid all the stresses she had to deal with following the murders, was questioned extensively by the authorities on, of all things, her little sister's underwear habits.

In addition to the out-of-place tire iron, investigators found in the van a Soda Springs trail map, a Mobil Oil Co. gas receipt, the van's keys under the mat, John's wallet, some cough drops, a fishing weight, a handkerchief, a rubber whistle thought to belong to Sabrina, and a book of matches from the Sidney Hotel in Sidney, British Columbia. Nothing extraordinary, though the matchbook would eventually be of some interest to investigators.

More intriguing, and disturbing, was the condition of the things John and Sabrina loaded into the van the night they were abducted. For Andrea's birthday gifts, they purchased a book on horses and a blue, quilted bundle-up blanket — a sensible, thoughtful gift during an energy crisis with beleaguered President Jimmy Carter imploring the country to lower the thermostat.

John and Sabrina's killer(s) fiendishly ripped into the presents, discarding the cheerful Christmas wrapping throughout the van, a chilling affront to the holidays. As a joke, the young couple had playfully packaged the blanket inside a box within two larger ones. The blanket, plucked from the box and its plastic wrapping, was found in a bundle on the first seat behind the driver's captain-type chair. In perhaps the biggest oversight in a case with no shortage of them, authorities paid scant attention to the blanket after it was found. It would ultimately be far and away the most important piece of evidence in the case.

The van and its contents yielded 64 fingerprints, 18 of them matching John and Sabrina and their families and friends. No footprints were detected in the van, even though the roads to the ravine were muddy. Speculation is that because John and Sabrina were found in a grassy/bushy area, their killer(s) walked only in this area, avoiding mud. No fingerprints were found on the three types of tape used to bind the victims, whose heads were sadistically wrapped like mummies, making it almost impossible to breathe (though both were alive at the time their throats were slashed as both inhaled blood into their lungs).

The tape used included both 2-inch and 1-inch silver duct tape, and half-inch filament tape. There was a piece of latex glove found on one bit of tape that either came from a murderer or the gloves of one of the pathologists while removing the considerable amounts of tape. Nobody knows for sure.

Kate Riggins had just cleaned the van a couple of days before her son's abduction. But she was never asked to look at it *before* it was cleaned out by investigators following the murders. The van, a horrific reminder of the tragedy, was sold by Riggins family friend Bruce Williams once investigators were through with it. (It is now reportedly scrap metal and of no use to investigators.)

"I knew what had been in there and I think if I had been allowed, I could have said, 'This isn't ours, or that isn't ours,'" recalled Kate, who believes she was not invited to look at the van because investigators didn't want to upset her.

"The fact that they didn't have my mom go and check out our van and say what belonged to them and what doesn't belong to them was kind of dumb," Carrie Riggins added. "Because there was stuff in the van that was ours, but then there was stuff in the van that wasn't ours. The van was impounded — and that was the last it was seen."

Also found in the van in a tipped-over brown paper grocery sack were three cartons of melted Lady Lee Ice Cream for the birthday party, a bargain brand sold in Davis exclusively at the Lucky supermarket the Gonsalves girls frequented. These three innocuous-looking cartons of ice cream, thoughtfully placed in a sack along with sprinkle toppings by Sabrina, would be of enormous importance.

12
Ice Cream

For years after Sabrina Gonsalves was so brutally and senselessly slain, her mother simply could not bring herself to have anything to do with what normally is a cheerful treat synonymous with special occasions.

"I couldn't look at ice cream," Kim Gonsalves said. "It made me sick to see it, to think about it."

You can't blame her. In one way or another, it was ice cream that likely cost Sabrina and John their lives. Walking hand in hand into the dense fog after working as ushers at the children's production of "The Davis Children's Nutcracker" at the Davis Veterans' Memorial Center, John and Sabrina climbed into John's van to go to Andrea's surprise birthday party at oldest sister Terese's apartment.

But first they drove to Sabrina's condo a mile away. There, they stopped to gather the presents and ice cream for the party. Sabrina also brought in the mail for a neighbor who was away. The condo stop may not have been necessary had it not been for the ice cream, which could have melted had it been left in the van during "The Nutcracker."

There were three flavors needed for the party: coffee, vanilla and rocky road. According to police, Terese purchased two half-gallons of ice cream for the party earlier in the week (it was on special at Lucky for $2.24 a half-gallon) and stored them in the condo's freezer. Neither flavor, however, was vanilla — birthday girl Andrea's favorite — prompting Sabrina to return to the store for the missing flavor.

So at some point, Sabrina bought a half-gallon of vanilla ice cream the day of the abductions at Lucky. The big question is when. The ice cream was found in an old brown grocery bag tipped over inside the van with an older Lucky receipt unrelated to the ice cream purchase. The vanilla was on top, put in the bag last. Although she never saw more than two half-gallons of ice cream in the freezer, Andrea told police that she thought Sabrina bought the vanilla before "The Nutcracker." If this is the case, John and Sabrina were

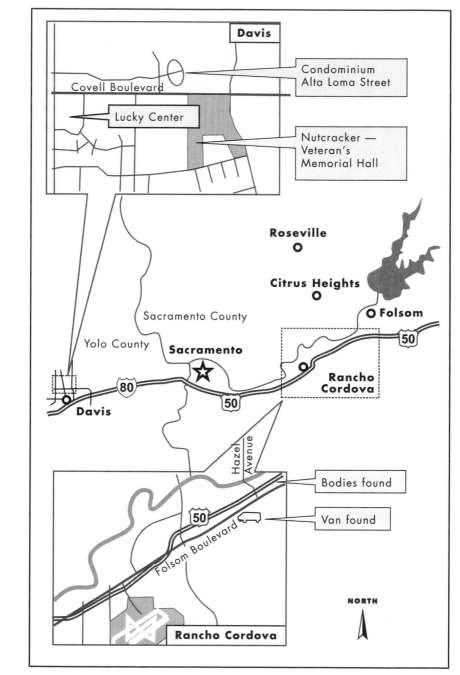

Davis

Condominium
Alta Loma Street

Covell Boulevard

Lucky Center

Nutcracker —
Veteran's
Memorial Hall

Roseville
O

Citrus Heights
O

O Folsom

Sacramento County

Yolo County

Sacramento

Rancho
Cordova

80

50

Davis

Hazel
Avenue

Bodies found

50

Van found

Folsom Boulevard

Rancho Cordova

NORTH

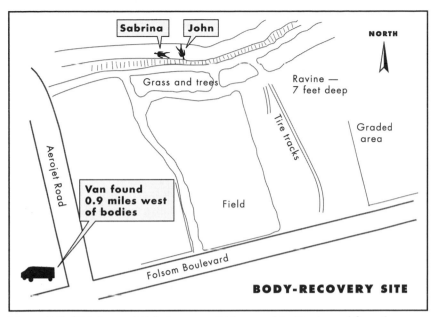

Figure 1 (left) John and Sabrina were kidnapped in Davis and found murdered in Rancho Cordova. Figure 2 (above) Detail of site where the bodies were found.

Maps by Joel Swift

likely abducted in the inky-dark, labyrinthine parking lot at the condo, to this day a spooky place at night. Then-Davis police officer Mark Safarik, now a profiler with the FBI, wrote a police report on April 4, 1982, suggesting John and Sabrina drove to the condo, collected the neighbor's mail and set it on the couch by the door. This suggests they were in a hurry to get to the party as Sabrina put the mail in a hall closet on previous days.

The sweethearts then grabbed all the ice cream from the condo freezer and put it in the bag with the old receipt. Shannon, Sabrina's fiercely protective German shepherd, stood guard inside the condo at the time, so it's highly unlikely the abduction took place indoors, as family members all agree Shannon would have ripped to shreds anyone who tried to attack Sabrina, or died trying.

John liked to park his family's van next to a secluded hedge a couple of condos away from Sabrina's. Safarik believes that because there was a lot to carry for the party, including the large box-within-boxes containing the quilted blanket, John and Sabrina left the condo together, popped open the back of the van and, with their backs turned, loaded the gifts and ice cream.

"At this time, both were overpowered and taken from the location," Safarik theorizes in his report.

While this theory is logical, the more popular theory — the one that was commonly accepted in Davis lore to the point that most people who remember the crime simply accept it as fact — is that John and Sabrina were taken at the Lucky shopping center on the way to Terese's birthday party.

Proponents of this theory believe they have eyewitness accounts on their side.

Following immense media attention in the days after the murders, which included plenty of TV and front-page photos of the victims (Davis was also papered with fliers describing the missing couple), witnesses came forward who were at the Lucky shopping center that night. A cook at the Chandelier restaurant on the shopping center's east side claimed to have seen John and Sabrina laughing at a menu in front of the restaurant.

"You should have seen them," the cook told The Sacramento Bee. "They were giggling and laughing. I asked them what they were laughing about, and they said they were laughing because the menu was so big." (Sabrina's family and others have doubts about this sighting, saying the couple were in too much of a hurry to look at a menu on the opposite end of the shopping center from Lucky). The cook also told The Bee he saw a suspicious man lingering about 20 feet from Riggins' van when he got off work sometime before 9 p.m.

"The guy was dressed in black, with a dark cap. When he saw me he looked away like he didn't want me to see him. It's real dark out there, so I didn't get a good look."

Roger Romani, a UC Davis professor, and two of his daughters picked up a pizza at the Chandelier around 8:30 p.m. The older daughter, Rebecca Romani, who went to high school with John Riggins, noticed two suspicious men lingering in a breezeway around 8:30 p.m. Like the cook, Romani noted that one of the men wore a knit cap.

In what was ultimately deemed the most reliable sighting of all at the time by authorities, a Lucky assistant manager/clerk told police he actually saw Sabrina and John at his checkstand about 8:30 p.m. The store employee said he recognized Sabrina as a regular customer, and gave a fairly accurate description of what she wore. But he described the woman's male companion as blond and wearing a jacket and tie; John Riggins had distinct red hair (though it was blondish at times, usually in the summer) and wore a brown sweater the night he was abducted.

The victims' families have differing theories on the kidnapping site and how the two were abducted. The Rigginses have doubts about the shopping center — John's mother, Kate, told me on a number of occasions that she believes they could just have easily been abducted at Terese's West Davis apartment complex, site of the birthday party. (No witnesses have put the van or the sweethearts in this area, though Sacramento County Homicide Detective Stan Reed said he thought it possible. He and Kate point to the fact that Terese's apartment complex is closer to a freeway exit for an assailant coming from the Bay Area.)

The Rigginses also believe John was friendly enough that if someone approached him in his hometown and duped him by pretending to be a stranded motorist he would not have hesitated to help. The Gonsalveses accepted the Lucky abduction-site theory as it became more popular with investigators. But Sabrina, they say, was brought up by a military man who worked with criminals, and she was raised to be very wary about helping strangers.

"They had ice cream in the car, and they had to get to the birthday party; they wouldn't have let themselves be delayed," Sabrina's father, George, maintained. "The (killers) would have had to be inside the van before they got back in the van, or a guy came to the van with a gun in his hand. That's the only way. Sabrina was sensitive. She would have been on the alert."

The slayings' immense media attention resulted in hundreds of tips to authorities, many of them noting a sighting of the Riggins van the night of the kidnapping, as well as a blue sedan. Ultimately, authorities whittled them down to a handful of reliable sightings.

Between 8:30 and 9 p.m., a Davis motorist idled on the east side of the Covell Boulevard overpass at a well-lighted bus stop near L Street waiting for a friend's car to catch up. This area is about a half-mile from Sabrina's condo and a mile from Lucky. After the motorist's friend caught up and passed him, the motorist moved back into the traffic lane and checked his rear-view mirror.

Barreling down the overpass came the Riggins' van, which swerved to the left to avoid hitting the startled driver. The man told authorities that he noticed what he believed were three people in the front of the van — a driver and a passenger in the two captain's chairs, and a third person in between. This witness could not determine the gender of the trio, though he thought one of them had long hair and one wore a cap, possibly a baseball hat.

He also said he saw two smaller cars trailing the van closely, one of them a blue sedan.

This overpass sighting, which seems reliable because the witness ID'd the van's personalized "3S MUM" license plate, shows that the killer(s) were on a route from either Lucky or Sabrina's condo heading east to a second Davis overpass (Mace Boulevard), where they could then get on the freeway to Sacramento.

Entering Interstate 80 from the Mace overpass, the van headed east over the fog-draped Yolo Causeway. Here another motorist spotted the van, a Sacramento man returning from the Bay Area with a friend. This witness told authorities that he saw a van driving erratically in the eastbound lane (toward Sacramento) about 9 p.m.

"I saw a van weaving, and it went over and hit the shoulder and came back, almost came over in the second lane," he said. "It looked like a sheet or a blanket or something was around the (driver's side) of the window. So I kind of stayed with it, kind of watching it, it weaved again, and it went back over and hit the shoulder and slowed down. So I stayed with it a little bit, and I figured maybe the person driving might have been sleepy or something."

This witness did not get a look at the van's driver or its occupants. John and Sabrina were undergoing an unimaginable period of terror at this time. The van swerving and the blanket covering a window indicated *something*. Maybe this is when John fought back, causing the driver to swerve, or when Sabrina was sexually assaulted. The blanket, found in the bench seat immediately behind the driver's chair, suggests something or someone was being covered up.

The next reliable sighting of the van came when John and Sabrina were being driven to the ravine 34 miles east of Davis. Following dinner at a Chinese restaurant, Carl White, a young Sacramento-area man, and his date headed to a lovers' lane, familiar to White, who grew up in the area. The parking spot was about a half-mile from the ravine where the bodies were found. As they enjoyed a glass of wine in the back of the van in the secluded spot, they were jolted out of their Saturday night coziness. Suddenly, White's van was illuminated by a shaky beam of light growing bigger by the second as it shone through the window. It was the Riggins van speeding toward them on a bumpy dirt road off Folsom Boulevard.

Fearing a collision, White climbed to the front of his van and flipped on his fog lights. He had about two seconds to notice a lone male in the driver's seat of the Riggins van, which then drove toward the ravine. White killed his lights. He eyed the van warily as its headlights were shut off after it backed up to the ravine behind some trees.

It was an ominous moment: This may have been when John and Sabrina were taken outside the van, their throats slit, the tape binding their limbs cut to make them easier to move, and then thrown, kicked or rolled into the ditch. (No blood was found in the van aside from a red smudge that may or may not have been blood, so it follows that they were killed where they were found.)

Seeing the eerie glow of the brake lights from the Riggins van as it backed into the ditch, White was overcome with a "weird feeling." He grabbed a shotgun that he kept in his own van, loaded it, had his date return to the passenger seat, and promptly left the area. He called the police after seeing the missing van on the TV news the night after the abduction.

There were more van sightings in the area after the time authorities believe the bodies were dumped. The blue sedan, seen by the overpass motorist in Davis, was later observed with the van by two independent witnesses in Sacramento, first at 10:55 p.m. when it was parked by the van on Hazel Avenue, then driving with the van on Sunrise Boulevard about 1 a.m. The blue sedan and the van may have bumped each other because a faint trace of blue paint was detected on the van's bumper.

Two additional sightings of the van occurred around Rudy's Hideaway, a supper club about a mile to the west that was packed that night with holiday parties. Joyce Hullender, a Sacramento woman driving home from an office Christmas party, noticed the Riggins van partially blocking the road in front of Rudy's, about a mile from the ravine. Both front doors were open, the lights and motor on.

Perturbed that the road was partially blocked, Hullender stepped out of her car and peered inside the van, its illuminated interior an eerie contrast to the misty December darkness shrouding Folsom Boulevard. She saw Christmas wrapping strewn about the van, and a baseball cap on one of the front seats, the second time a witness recalled seeing a baseball cap in the van.

"I just looked in it and I heard footsteps in the fog and I got out of there, because I was doing something I wasn't supposed to be doing; I had my head in someone else's car," Hullender would later say.

Frightened, she left when the footsteps turned out to be those of a man getting into the van.

Also seen that night by a lone female motorist was a man walking near

**Police composite of a man in
bloody T-shirt seen emerging
from bushes near the
body-dump site.**

Rudy's. And two suspicious-looking men coming out of a field by Rudy's
were observed by Robert and Audrey Reid, an older couple who had just
finished eating there.

"How's it going?" Robert Reid asked the two men after they emerged from
the foggy field.

No response.

The following morning, a motorist eastbound on Highway 50, told authorities she saw a man near the ravine where the bodies were dumped around 9 a.m.
He wore a yellow, blood-stained T-shirt. He was described as white, between
22 and 26, up to about 6 feet 2 inches tall with shaggy or feathered hair parted
down the middle. This man was seen along Highway 50 near an eastbound
offramp to Folsom Boulevard, just east of the Aerojet Road offramp.

Sacramento Sheriff's Department Homicide Bureau Supervisor Lt. Ray
Biondi told the media in 1981 that the witness saw the man, reportedly
wearing a yellow, blood-stained T-shirt, emerge from some bushes along the
highway and enter a dark-brown standard-size pickup truck. "It appeared
he was waiting for this particular vehicle, according to the witness," Biondi
said. "The vehicle came and he just got right in."

A second white male adult drove the pickup, indicating that the killer had
an accomplice. Like much of the evidence in this case, this sighting eventually fell through the cracks.

13
Who?

Riggins-Gonsalves was a high-profile case, the kind any detective loved solving. In the weeks following Dec. 20, 1980, detectives from both the Sacramento County Sheriff's Department's homicide unit and the Davis Police Department doggedly worked the double-homicide of a surgeon's son and an Army lieutenant colonel's daughter. Because Sacramento County had more experience investigating homicides — the county in the early 1980s had up to 50 homicides a year; it was a busy year for Davis if it had more than one — it was decided that the sheriff's department would take the lead in the case.

It is a decision some in Davis law enforcement would ultimately regret as Sacramento detectives became saddled with new homicides and spent less time on the case. With no motive, hardly any evidence, no suspects, and hundreds of tips, most of them fruitless, there were all kinds of names and theories floating around. "Channeling" from psychics was even used, but led to nothing useful. Some witnesses were even hypnotized.

Theories ranged from the slayings being a part of a sadistic cult ritual because they occurred the weekend of the 1980 winter solstice, to the killer(s) seeking to settle a score with Sabrina's father over his work in prisons or the military. There was even speculation that attractive, vivacious Andrea Gonsalves, who had been in Davis longer than her roommate-sister, was the intended target — and that the killer confused her with Sabrina.

"They actually went and interviewed jilted boyfriends of mine," Andrea said. "And a professor I turned in for sexual harassment. They thought maybe he had a vendetta. Police went knocking on his door."

Nothing came of it.

Among the early leads that held some promise was Henry Cook,* a convicted rapist who had a turbulent relationship with a UC Davis law student. When the law student tried to break off the relationship, Cook got physical with her. When her brother interceded, Cook stabbed him in the chest. Despite Cook's violent history, investigators could never build a credible case against him.

---

*The names of some people in this book have been changed. Such names are denoted by an asterisk (*) the first time each appears in the book.

Other noteworthy possibilities emerged. On Jan. 11, 1981 — about three weeks after the murders — Kevin Thorpe, 21, and Laura Craig, 20, were bound for Oregon from their Ridgecrest, Calif., home when, like John and Sabrina, they apparently were simply in the wrong place at the wrong time.

Driving through the tiny Lassen County town of Madeline (about 300 miles northeast of Davis), the couple stopped at a café/service station for gas.

Eyeing them lustfully in a yellow pickup were Benjamin Wai Silva, 28, Norman Thomas, 20 and Joseph Shelton, 28. Acting on a prearranged plan to kidnap a woman to be a sex slave, the three men followed the unsuspecting couple. Posing as police officers, they duped the sweethearts into pulling over by flashing a red spotlight. They abducted the terrified couple at gunpoint, taking them to Shelton's cabin 7 miles from Madeline, where they chained Kevin Thorpe to a tree. Shelton then shot him with a machine gun and ordered Thomas to hack up Thorpe's body and bury it in shallow graves.

Thomas, Shelton and Silva then took turns raping and torturing Laura Craig over the next four days. Thomas, who confessed to his role in the crime after being arrested for a separate burglary, told authorities Shelton and Silva killed Craig after taking her with them to a rural location and raping her some more before shooting her in the head and dumping her over an embankment.

All three men were arrested not long after the heinous crimes. Thomas testified against Silva and Shelton. Shelton was sentenced to life without parole in December 1981, Silva was sentenced to death in March 1982, but an appeals court reversed the death sentence in 2002, saying Silva had ineffective counsel.

Investigators working the Riggins-Gonsalves slayings became interested in the Lassen County murders when, on Jan. 1981, Davis police received a call from a student enrolled in UC Davis' renowned school of veterinary medicine. The student said she knew both Shelton and Andrea Gonsalves' boyfriend (now husband), Steve Rosenstein, also a vet student. The tipster said prior to the Lassen murders, Shelton had been in the Sacramento area on Dec. 19, the day before John and Sabrina's abduction. Sacramento County homicide detectives declined to pursue the Shelton-Silva lead after interrogating Shelton in jail following his arrest for the Lassen murders and staking out a Sacramento residence he was known to visit.

Another lead, one especially popular with the late Davis police Detective Bob Persons, one of the first detectives to work the case, explored a connection between an ex-Davisite and John Riggins. In one of the more dramatic crimes in Davis history, two Davis brothers, John and Michael Abbott, robbed a downtown jewelry store in 1976. Following the robbery, Michael Abbott, 18, was killed in a gunfight with Davis police. The Abbotts lived with their mother, Ursula Abbott, a famous UC Davis avian scientist, and John Riggins was once their paperboy — and was afraid to collect money because, he told his family, the Abbotts had an "attack rooster." Not only that, but John resembled Michael Abbott, who, like John, had red hair and fair skin.

For years, Persons obsessed over John Abbott being behind the Riggins-Gonsalves slayings because Abbott wanted to avenge his brother's death by getting back at Davis by killing someone who resembled his younger brother — in this case John Riggins. Michael Abbott graduated with the Davis High class of 1975, which, on Dec. 20, 1980, held a reunion at the Davis Veterans Memorial Center — the same building whose main auditorium housed the "Nutcracker" production that John and Sabrina worked that night.

The big problem with the Abbott theory is that John Abbott was in jail on Dec. 20, 1980, in Canada on charges stemming from his involvement in a November 1980 shootout with Royal Canadian Mounties. He was not even in the same country as John and Sabrina the night they were abducted.

But because Abbott was known as a manipulator and con artist, authorities believed it possible that he could have ordered an acquaintance in the Bay Area, Phillip Thompson, a criminal with a record of violence, to kill John and Sabrina. Abbott's trail cooled after detectives interviewed Thompson and could find nothing to connect either man to the killings. Later — much later — there would be renewed interest in him.

Investigators also checked out but could not build a case against Ward Francis Weaver Jr., an Oroville truck driver who was facing trial for two murders in Kern County and was a suspect in several rapes and murders in other states. Also questioned was David Carpenter, the "Trailside Killer" convicted of murders in Marin and Santa Cruz counties, including the March 1981 killing of Davis resident Ellen Hansen in a park near Santa Cruz. Carpenter also shot and wounded Hansen's boyfriend, Davisite Steven Haertle, whose testimony against Carpenter led to his conviction and death sentence in 1984. (At this writing, Carpenter is still on California's Death Row.)

Detectives additionally took a long look and ultimately eliminated drifter Henry Lee Lucas, who in 1983 claimed to have committed hundreds of murders, including the 1977 stabbing death of Elizabeth Mary Wolf at her West

Davis apartment. It is now believed that Lucas confessed to the Wolf slaying and other murders to delay his execution for the few murders for which he was convicted.

Other leads were explored. The murder of Sabrina and John occurred a mere 48 days after Mary Beth Sowers and Craig Miller were slain after being abducted from the Arden Fair Mall parking lot in Sacramento. There were grim similarities: Attractive white college couples; both abducted on a weekend night; at least one, and perhaps both couples, taken from a Sacramento-area shopping center; bodies dumped in plain view in remote areas.

The only problem was the suspected killer of Miller and Sowers, Gerald Gallego, 34, was already in jail when Sabrina and John were killed. "See, I didn't do it – the killer is still out there!" Gallego told his jailers just days after the murders. By Dec. 29, Gallego's lawyers were filing discovery motions seeking information in the Riggins-Gonsalves case to bolster Gallego's defense that he was not responsible for the Miller-Sowers slayings.

A Sacramento County sheriff's spokesman told reporters in January 1981 that so far, the investigation of the Davis slayings had unearthed no link to the Sacramento State couple. But the similarities were not lost on the media. The Sacramento Bee, for one, noted as early as Dec. 28, a week after the Davis couple were killed, that, "Several people have suggested that someone decided to copy the murders of Miller and Sowers."

At least three men familiar with Gerald Gallego reportedly told authorities that Gallego's slightly older, fiercely loyal half-brother, David Hunt, 36, might be involved in the Riggins-Gonsalves slayings. Hunt, a career criminal who some considered more vicious than Gallego, had been paroled from San Quentin on Oct. 14, 1980.

On Dec. 24, a Sacramento County Jail inmate aware of the Davis murders, wrote a letter to then-Sheriff Duane Lowe suggesting Hunt was involved in the highly publicized killings. On Dec. 30, an investigator working out of Folsom Prison contacted homicide detective Stan Reed and said he thought Hunt may have committed a copycat murder.

In late January, Ray Lopez,* a longtime police informant who grew up with Hunt and Gallego in Sacramento's gritty Oak Park neighborhood, eyed a sketch in The Bee of a white man with wild eyes and a prominent nose, features he thought resembled Hunt's. The sketch, which ran in several California newspapers, was based on the newspaper deliveryman's eyewitness account of seeing a man in a bloody T-shirt enter a pickup the morning after the murders. Seeking reward money from The Bee's Secret Witness Program, Lopez called the Sacramento Sheriff's Department and reported that he believed Hunt committed the murders. It would not be the last time Ray Lopez would thrust himself into this case.

As head of the Sacramento County homicide detectives, Lt. Ray Biondi knew of David Hunt's ties to Gallego as he focused most of his attention at that time on Gallego's many murders. But without any direct evidence linking Hunt to the crime, Gallego's half-brother became just one of many leads.

Hunt, wanted for his role in breaking Richard Thompson out of San Quentin on Nov. 24, 1980, was arrested on Feb. 19, 1981, in Chico while visiting his and Gallego's mother, Lorraine Davies. While Hunt remained on the lam for the escape, his and Thompson's pictures were circulated at Gallego's Sacramento courthouse hearings because authorities feared the two fugitives would try yet another daring escape — busting Gerald Gallego out of custody.

Following Hunt's arrest for helping Thompson escape (Thompson was arrested a few weeks earlier in Southern California), Sacramento Detective Stan Reed contacted Hunt in person on March 4, 1981, about two and a half months after the Davis murders. Hunt declined to be interviewed, telling Reed that he could not say where he was the night Sabrina and John were abducted because such information might be used against him on his pending escape charges — though Hunt did say, "I didn't do it," and, "I could never kill a young girl."

"He wouldn't talk to us," Reed recalled. "He said, 'I'm on parole. When I get off parole, you get a hold of me and I'll talk to you.' That was the end of that — he wouldn't talk to me."

On April 6, 1982, Reed again phoned Hunt. This time, Hunt claimed that throughout December 1980, he was living in some low-rent apartments in Phoenix, Ariz., with his new wife, Suellen.

Hunt would not be questioned about the Riggins-Gonsalves murders again until 1987.

Joel Davis

Who?

14
Profiler

While there were scores of tips and leads in the aftermath of the Riggins-Gonsalves murders, investigators were never close to solving the case in the weeks, months, and even years after Dec. 20, 1980. There was no motive. No weapon. Scant evidence. No leading suspects. The trail grew so cold that the Rigginses considered hiring a private investigator.

Meanwhile, other cases piled up for the Sacramento sheriff's homicide unit. Investigators hardly forgot about Riggins-Gonsalves, but over time it became one of many unsolved murders in a county that, on average, had almost a murder a week throughout the 1980s.

"We had other murders," Detective Stan Reed said of the months following Sabrina and John's killings. "We had a lot of stuff going on. But (Riggins-Gonsalves) was worked. I don't think it was extra busy (in the months following the killings), but it was certainly busy enough. My plate was full."

Months melted into years. Sabrina's parents moved to Tacoma, Wash., John's to Atlanta, where Dr. Riggins got a job at Emory University and a new start far from a town that was a constant reminder of horror.

But the case was far from forgotten in Davis, where concerned citizens — led by close Riggins family friend Dr. Andrew Gabor, a renowned neurologist — in 1981 formed a grassroots patrol against crime that ultimately fizzled out when it was realized that the murders were simply an aberration in the placid college town.

But the killings lingered in the minds of the local police, piquing the interest of young Davis Police Detective Mark Safarik. A UC Davis graduate, Safarik was a patrol officer when John and Sabrina were killed. Tall, educated, handsome and imposing, he soon was promoted to detective. Not long after taking on his new post, he decided to give the Riggins-Gonsalves case a look. "Basically, it wasn't going anywhere," Safarik said. "They didn't have any suspects. They had nothing, and no leads were coming in."

During this time, Safarik attended a two-week "homicide school" featur-

Mark Safarik, circa 2002
Mark Safarik

ing three FBI profilers.

"I had a couple of days of instruction by the profilers, and I was absolutely fascinated by it, hooked," said Safarik, who went on to become a profiler for the FBI, where he still works. "I thought this case would be a good case to have assessed since it wasn't going anywhere."

In 1983 Safarik got FBI profiler Ron Walker to look at the case. The Riggins-Gonsalves FBI profile is what's known as a basic profile. Such composites take existing police reports and photographs, compare them to similar cases, and, using probabilities, predict an assailant's race, gender, age, intelligence, education, work habits and relationships. More thorough profiles are performed when a killer strikes repeatedly and leaves "signature" evidence. In these cases, the profiler typically visits the crime scene in person, something that was not done in this case, though Safarik forwarded to the profiler details from his visits to the body-dump site, including his supposition that the killer(s) knew just where they were going on Dec. 20, 1980.

"I went to the (murder) scene at night to see what conditions these offenders had to work in," Safarik noted. "At that time it was so isolated, you couldn't have found it unless you knew where it was. It was not even really a road, it was just a little dirt trail along a fence, sort of out in the country and was pitch black out there. You wouldn't have found it by accident."

After studying the information, Walker submitted the following profile:

Victimology

"John Riggins and Sabrina Gonsalves appear to have been mature, well-adjusted college students with supportive, comfortable family backgrounds. Neither victim is suspected of drug experimentation or excessive alcohol use, and both were athletically inclined. They cared deeply for each other and were described by friends as pleasant, friendly, and easy to get along with; they seem to have had no enemies. Their background would indicate that they are very low-risk victims of violent crime, and could correspondingly be seen as victims of opportunity in this instance. However, analysis of the crime scene appears to indicate that one of the victims, most probably Sabrina Gonsalves, may well have been known to the assailant, perhaps not on a close, personal basis, but likely as a passing acquaintance or as a "familiar face in the neighborhood.""

Offense

"Review of the medical examiner's report and of the submitted photographs indicates both victims were bound with duct and/or filament tape. Both received incised neck wounds, with the male victim suffering blunt force head wounds. Cause of death appears to have been neck wounds (incised)/aspiration of blood. Asphyxiation due to the female taping of her entire head is also significant. Neither victim appears to have been sexually assaulted. However, Sabrina Gonsalves did suffer some vaginal mucosal abrasions and roughening.

The overall impression of the offense data indicates an assailant who is intelligent, adaptive and methodical."

Crime Analysis

"The victims are believed to have been accosted and abducted from the parking lot of Gonsalves' (condominium). Since both victims were athletic and strong, the initial approach/assault by the offender caught them by surprise. The offender probably aroused no suspicion on the victims' part since he may have been recognized by one or the other. The assailant, having to establish control over two individuals, would then have displayed a weapon (bladed instrument), probably threatening initially the female victim. After forcing the victims into their van, the assailant then would have assaulted the male victim with a blunt instrument to further maintain control. The victims would then have been taped using available duct and filament tape. The blunt-force assault to the male, coupled with the care the assailant took to bind both victims, indicates a great deal of caution on his part. It also indicates the assailant acted alone.

Two assailants, due to their ability to physically control the victims, would not find it necessary to bind the victims in this manner. The failure of the assailant to tape the female victim's legs indicates he probably intended to sexually assault her.

In fact, this profiler believes that the intended sexual assault of Sabrina Gonsalves was the motive for the attack. The assailant may well have digitally manipulated Gonsalves' genital area, resulting in the superficial roughening and mucosal abrasion described by the medical examiner. The assailant, having taped his victims, then drove to a remote lovers' lane area known to him. At this point he may have discovered that due to the severity of Sabrina Gonsalves' taping she may have lapsed into unconsciousness due to partial asphyxiation. The assailant now had no choice but to kill the victims and dispose of the bodies. This profiler believes that the assailant cut the tapes securing John Riggins, led him to the area of the ravine, and cut his throat.

Riggins is seen as the first victim due to the numerous superficial cuts on his throat, which are indicative of hesitation marks. Sabrina Gonsalves, the second victim, was incised with much more assurance and confidence. These facts would also indicate that this assailant has not killed prior to this instance.

The victims were literally dumped into the ravine by the assailant, and the van was abandoned about one mile away. The location of the van, as well as the way in which the victims were disposed of, indicates the assailant either wanted them found or did not care if they were discovered. The sighting of the van at the roadside establishment that night indicates that the assailant very likely stopped to place a phone call to an associate, since he required a ride back to Sacramento/Davis. It is believed that the assailant resides in that area."

Offender Profile

"The offender in this case is seen as an adaptive, intelligent individual. His initial motive was sexual assault. He was able to gain complete control over the victims relatively easily, using a personal weapon as well as implements available to him that belonged to the victims.

This offender is a white male between 23 to 28 years of age. This crime scene dictates an experienced, reasoning, methodical offender. He is of above-average intelligence, and will be a high school graduate. He may well have attended college classes as well. In school, he was active athletically, probably in individual-type sports, i.e., wrestling, swimming, etc. He is muscular and takes pride in his appearance. He is described by his associates as self-centered and manipulative. His associates will very likely be significantly younger (17-20 years old).

The offender is known to carry weapons and has displayed those weapons in a threatening or boastful manner to others. He may well have a history of assaultive behavior, particularly against women. He does date, and may well have a girlfriend. This female is seen as a subservient-type individual. He may well have a military history, probably Army or Marine Corps. While in the military he will have had discipline problems and may have received a general or dishonorable discharge.

The offender resides or works in the vicinity of the Davis campus or near Sabrina Gonsalves' residence. Although the offender may not have had a personal relationship with Gonsalves, he very likely knew her as a neighbor or "familiar face in the neighborhood." This is supported by the depersonalization evident in the manner that her entire face was covered in duct tape."

Post-Offense Behavior

"Immediately after the crime, the assailant very probably became withdrawn and preoccupied; this would have been noticed by those close to him. He may well have suffered some initial guilt since he did not set out to commit murder. However, the time that has passed since the commission of the offense has allowed him to cope with his acts. It is also likely that the assailant left the area, but not immediately after the offense. It is also possible due to a lack of concrete evidence and a failure to solve this homicide, the offender may have returned to the Sacramento/Davis area.

Of significance in this case is that the assailant involved an unwitting individual in the post-offense aspect of this murder. Having abandoned the victims' van, the assailant may very likely have contacted an associate by telephone to request a ride back to the Davis area. This individual was probably a girlfriend or younger male associate of the assailant, and was totally unaware of the assailant's acts. An excellent investigative lead, therefore, would be a request through the local media for this individual to come forward. This profiler strongly believes that such a second, unwitting person was involved since the assailant would not risk hitchhiking for fear of identification. It is also believed that the assailant disposed of the murder weapon almost immediately after the homicide, most likely somewhere along the route back toward the Sacramento area.

The assailant, described as intelligent and adaptive, no longer harbors feelings of guilt and remorse. His greatest concern is fear of discovery. If interviewed, he will be overly cooperative; it is very possible that he was already interviewed during the initial stages of the investigation. If polygraphed, test results will be inconclusive."

While this profile was released to the media and was heavily publicized, it led to no promising leads or suspects. Safarik stands behind it, though he has some questions of his own. For starters, he wonders why the culprit(s) went to all the trouble and risk of transporting John and Sabrina 35 miles.

"If your intent is to kill them, just kill them. Why do you have to take them in their van? You could have driven three minutes from where they live out in just as vacant of county land at that time, right off of Covell Boulevard. But why did you have to elevate your risk by driving all the way over to the other side of Sacramento? Why not take them in your car instead of in their van? That van is pretty recognizable. It's got personalized plates, it's a big thing that you are not going to miss."

The profile described a "careful" assailant, but Safarik thinks otherwise.

"How do you know you are not going to get stopped by the CHP when you are driving across on the causeway late at night? Good lord, you got two people bound up in the van. I mean, it's very high-risk."

Safarik believed Sabrina and John likely were victims of opportunity who didn't know their killer(s). He found it odd that John, athletic, strong and protective, was taken along with Sabrina. "It's very high-risk to take the male. If Sabrina was the target, then the question is why doesn't he wait until Sabrina is alone?

"That means he really wants to offend, badly. He has a reason that he needs to offend, and he's willing to take the risk of assaulting and abducting two able-bodied people. And killing both of them."

The crime scene also strikes Safarik as unusual, namely the positioning of Riggins' van, found with its keys under the driver's side floor mat.

"The killer doesn't intend to take it anywhere or do anything with the van because it's only found less than a mile from the scene. Why doesn't he just leave it there, walk out on the road, and get his ride from whoever he needs to get the ride from?

"But that's not what happened. Instead, subsequent to the homicide, this guy elevates his risk by getting back in the van, driving it onto the road where he could be seen driving to that location and could be seen parking on that side of the road, where the van clearly will be found...it could have been driven into Folsom Lake, and nobody would have found the van. They could have driven it up into cliffs up at Tahoe and just driven it off the hundreds of steep ravines up there.

"They could have driven it a lot of places. But that's not what they do. What they do is they drive it a very short distance away, and they park it right next to the road; then, to make sure that nobody else steals it, they lock it up with the keys. Clearly the offender realizes the kids are going to be found missing, very shortly because it's nighttime, and there's going to be somebody looking for that van, and lo and behold, here it is sitting right next to side of the road.

"Once you look at the van and you see the mud all over the tires, it isn't going to take a rocket scientist to figure out you need to start looking in the area where the van was found. And that's exactly what they did, and then they find the bodies."

While the profiling posed some interesting questions in this case, and would seem remarkably prescient two decades later, it still didn't lead to any immediate answers. Lt. Ray Biondi, supervisor of Sacramento County's investigation of the case after the murders occurred, is skeptical about profiling, though he said it can help because it gives detectives another way to look at crime scenes.

"Profilers are much like psychics wherein you (only) hear about what turned out to be correct in the profile," Biondi noted. "There is not much publicity about all the profiles that were totally off-base. You certainly do not eliminate a suspect because he did not fit the profile.

"An experienced homicide detective is a 'profiler' in that he knows what kind of person would commit a particular murder. Plus he has the benefit of all his senses by experiencing the crime scene/autopsy/investigation.

"Murders," Biondi maintained, "are solved by getting off your ass and knocking on doors. Not by profiles."

Unfortunately, the number of doors being knocked on in the Riggins-Gonsalves case started diminishing in the early 1980s.

The case was cold.

15
Fred

Fred Turner has an everyman quality befitting the vagaries of detective work. Except for a set of beady eyes that seem more apt for the criminals he has pursued, Fred Turner is the kind of lawman who melts into the scenery.

He's about average height, with an average build, with medium-length brown hair and a complexion that is neither dark nor pale. His voice is like his appearance: pleasant, but not particularly distinct. He is neither laid-back nor excitable. His dress is between formal and casual. He drives a sensible American-made sedan, likes a turkey sandwich for lunch.

Fred Turner, in short, looks, acts, dresses and talks like a Fred Turner.

A native San Franciscan, Turner grew up on the Peninsula, where he developed a love for the ocean and big working ships. In the early 1960s, he earned a degree in agricultural business management from UC Davis. After college he took a job managing a large farm in dusty Fresno County. There, he got his first taste of police work, chasing down illegal hunters on farmland as a Fresno County constable. He then became a reserve officer with the tiny Mendota Police Department, where he once saved a 10-month-old from drowning.

In 1971, Turner joined the Davis Police Department as a rookie police officer and began a steady if unremarkable tenure with a department in a city in which violent crime is as rare as service calls are common. Although he wasn't directly assigned to it until 1987, the Riggins-Gonsalves case never left Turner's mind. A 37-year-old patrolman when John and Sabrina were killed, Turner was on duty the night the families hurried down to the police station to report Sabrina and John missing, sure they had not eloped. The department also assigned him to guard the Riggins home in the days after the bodies were discovered. He broke the grim news to John's parents that their son was found murdered.

Not long after the murders, Turner felt the pull of the sea. He left police work and the landlocked flatlands of Davis to attend merchant marine school in San

Fred Turner, circa 2000

Fred Turner

Francisco, which led to a sailor's job with the Masters Mates and Pilots Union.

Turner soon got engaged, and traded the sea for domestic life. He returned to the Davis Police Department in 1982 after two off-duty Davis policemen, John Stroble and John Hubert, were killed in a sailboating accident.

He remembered the Riggins-Gonsalves case, remembered how it left both the city of Davis and the university feeling violated. And he wanted to solve it.

Despite the slayings sending shockwaves through the Sacramento Valley, the Riggins-Gonsalves probe had gone cold by the mid-1980s. But in 1986, Sacramento Sheriff's Lt. Ray Biondi told Davis Police Lt. Steve Stout that he had an informant who believed David Hunt, Gerald Gallego's half brother, was behind the sweetheart murders. This same informant had first called authorities with the Hunt tip back in 1981. But this tip had been given scant notice amid the flurry of other leads.

Now, with the case going nowhere, it was worth a second look, especially because the informant had called Biondi incessantly, even showed up on his doorstep several times, adamant that Hunt was responsible.

While a reluctant-to-talk Hunt had been briefly questioned about the killings twice in the early 1980s by Sacramento homicide Detective Stan Reed, the fact that Ray Lopez,* viewed as a reliable paid informant on stolen goods and other nickel-and-dime cases, was involved, renewed interest in Hunt.

Working with a Sacramento burglary investigator, Lopez, a small, wiry, light-skinned Hispanic no bigger than a jockey, would sell stolen stereos, VCRs and other hot goods to Sacramento-area crooks and fences, snaring them for the police in the process. He made $50 to $1,500 a case for his help. Although he had a lengthy criminal record of his own, Lopez was viewed as a reliable snitch.

"A detective for the city of Sacramento told me about Ray and sent Ray over to talk to me," Biondi said. "He'd used (Lopez) a lot in property cases and he'd been made reliable for search and arrest warrants."

Not only that, but Lopez knew Hunt and Gallego well. Very well. He grew up with them on the dangerous streets of Sacramento's Oak Park neighborhood, went to elementary school with them, and once even got arrested with Gallego for burglarizing a Chico gun store.

With the case stagnant, Biondi had an idea: Have Lopez buddy up to his old acquaintance Hunt and get a confession. Biondi knew of Hunt from his years as the lead lawman who brought Gallego to justice. Gallego, by this time on Nevada's Death Row, was convicted largely on the testimony of his wife and co-conspirator, Charlene, who cut a deal with prosecutors in exchange for a lighter sentence.

Charlene feared David Hunt.

"All the time we were interviewing Charlene, she was telling me about David Hunt," Biondi explained. "It was her opinion that the real violent person was David Hunt, not Gerald Gallego."

The search for Hunt intensified. One minor problem: In 1986, nobody had a clue of Hunt's whereabouts since 1984. Biondi ran Hunt's name through the usual criminal screenings, but had no luck locating him. In March 1987 Fred Turner, now interested in the case as a Davis police investigator, gave it a go. "I ran a federal rap sheet on David Hunt," Turner said. "Sacramento County never ran a federal rap sheet on him. I did. It took me all of about eight hours to find David Hunt."

Hunt, as it turns out, sat in federal prison in Lompoc in Central California the whole time Biondi and the Sacramento County Sheriff's Department looked for him. But in a communication breakdown between law agencies, Hunt could not be found.

Turner, fresh from an FBI workshop where he learned how to do federal searches for violent criminals using a new computer technology, ran Hunt's name. Hunt, Turner learned, was serving a 35-year federal sentence for a 1985 kidnapping of a young Washington couple who were taken by knife and bound with tape.

Young couple. Kidnapping. Knife. Tape.

Turner sat up in his chair. At long last, a possible break — hell, a huge break in his estimation — in this most baffling of cases. Turner ferreted out additional similarities between Hunt's June 21, 1985, kidnapping of a young couple, Steven Skuza and Kirsten Baugher, on federal land in Washington, and the kidnapping and murder of John and Sabrina on Dec. 20, 1980.

Skuza and girlfriend Baugher, who told authorities that Hunt raped her during the kidnapping, were abducted by Hunt and an accomplice over a drug deal gone bad. They were rescued after a federal policewoman patrolling Ft. Lewis happened upon them.

Turner compared the cases. Both involved young, attractive white sweethearts; a weekend night; vans being used to transport the victims; the male being beaten; tape and blindfolds used to restrain at least one of the victims; and knives used to control the victims in both cases.

"When I found out what David Hunt was in custody for, and I started looking at that crime, I saw so many similarities between that and Riggins-Gonsalves, I couldn't believe it," Turner said.

Turner dug deeper. He wanted to know precisely where David Hunt was on Dec. 20, 1980, the day John and Sabrina were kidnapped. Through the arrest and sentencing information on the Washington case, Turner learned that Hunt had a wife, Suellen Hunt. Turner had a fellow Davis investigator track down their marriage license. Once again, Turner could not believe what he found.

David and Suellen Hunt were wed between 1:30 p.m. and 2 p.m. the afternoon of Dec. 20, 1980. Not only that, but the wedding took place in Carson City, Nev. — a three-hour drive from Davis. Suddenly, Fred Turner not only had David Hunt committing a similar crime, but he also had him within striking distance of Davis on the night of the most shocking crime in city history. "It was the first indication I had that I could put these people 110 miles from the (murder)," Turner said.

It was time to put police informant Ray Lopez to work.

16
Snitch

"You put duct tape around your wrists, you ain't going to get out of it."

— Richard Thompson

From the moment the bodies were found, rewards were offered for information leading to the arrest and conviction of the killer or killers of John Riggins and Sabrina Gonsalves. The reward money poured in via private donations from Davisites, law agencies, the military through its association with Sabrina's family, and The Sacramento Bee's Secret Witness program. The total was upwards of $30,000.

Little Ray Lopez held odd jobs over the years: restaurant employee, Sheetrock hanger, laborer. But his main trade, his meal ticket dating back to 1969, was snitching on criminals. Given that most of his payoffs were well under $1,000, Lopez stood to hit the jackpot in the Riggins-Gonsalves case.

Lopez studied a composite sketch of the possible murder suspect that the Sacramento media published not long after the slayings. He had a hunch David Hunt was involved, Hunt's motive being a copycat killing to provide half-brother Gerald Gallego with an alibi. Both Hunt and the wild-eyed man in the police composite appeared to be the same age, had medium-to-dark hair and had a prominent nose — and Lopez thought he saw a resemblance.

With Hunt locked up in Lompoc, authorities had an idea: have Lopez visit Hunt, whom Lopez had known since elementary school. Perhaps he could get a confession or damning information.

Lt. Ray Biondi had tried more than once to get Lopez to squeeze information from Gallego, who, aided by his wife, Charlene, was believed to have killed as many as 10 people in sex-slave murders in the late 1970s and 1980. Charlene told Biondi that she helped Gallego abduct Brenda Lynne Judd, 14, and Sandra Kaye Colley, 13, from the Washoe County Fair in Reno in June 1979 so Gerald could sexually assault and kill them. But their bodies — key to building a case against Gallego for the Reno murders — could not be found.

**Richard Thompson, left, with David Hunt, right, and an unidentified man in a
San Quentin jail cell, circa 1980.**

Biondi, therefore, rigged Lopez up with a hidden tape recorder and sent
him on several occasions to visit Gallego in prison in Nevada to find out
where Gallego dumped the bodies. Lopez tried to dupe Gallego into talking
by saying he stood to gain a big reward by finding the bodies.

Gallego wasn't buying it. Although in chains, Gallego looked menacingly
at Lopez. "I can put these chains around your neck and kill you before the
guards could get in the room," he snarled.

In the wake of the unsuccessful attempts with Gallego, having Lopez try
to squeeze a confession out of Hunt in federal prison in Lompoc was deemed
both too risky and was met with resistance by officials there. So they settled
on the next best thing: Hunt's "road dog" — Richard Thompson.

A native of Colorado, Richard Harold Thompson, the second of five children, grew up in a stable family. Despite a relatively happy childhood, he
dropped out of high school in 10th grade, though he did complete high school
by taking equivalency courses after joining the Navy in 1952. By 1965 he had

been divorced twice and had two sons. Although he had skills as a carpenter, by 1967 Thompson was a career criminal who would ingest just about anything that got him high, especially heroin. In Southern California he was arrested several times for a variety of drug and weapons charges. Mainly nickel-and-dime stuff, but there were a few eye-openers: In 1974 Thompson was arrested for his part in an armed robbery of an appliance store and sentenced to state prison in Tehachapi, Calif. The following year, he and a fellow inmate broke out of that prison, but were soon caught in a stolen getaway car. In 1978 he was convicted of heroin possession; not long after he got out of jail for that, he pulled a gun on a couple in the parking lot of a Culver City Thrifty drugstore, stole their car, then robbed a supermarket cashier at gunpoint.

After being arrested for this robbery, Thompson was imprisoned in San Quentin, a notoriously tough state prison where he became a fast friend with fellow inmate David Hunt. When a freshly paroled Hunt helped his buddy Thompson make his prison breakout on Nov. 24, 1980, he did it with the help of Thompson's third wife, Valerie, and depending on whom you talk to, Hunt's then-girlfriend, Suellen (Suellen denies that she helped or knew of the escape). The friends then went on a multistate crime spree, but when they returned to California, Thompson was arrested for a burglary in Santa Monica on Jan. 28, 1981, and subsequently charged with the 1980 prison escape. He was shipped back to San Quentin in April 1981. He was paroled on May 5, 1987, to Los Angeles County. He had not seen David Hunt in years.

Pale, scrawny and with sharp facial features, Thompson was a smart prisoner and a dumb crook capable of heinous crimes. "He has established a concrete pattern of escapes from detention facilities," a probation officer noted. "This sophistication appears to cease immediately after the defendant is at liberty, in view of the fact that he has been apprehended within a relatively brief time after each episode. Consequently, it becomes apparent that Mr. Thompson is incapable of functioning in the community. Fortunately, he has not injured or killed anyone...during the commission of his crimes. The circumstances and nature of his threats during these crimes, however, do indicate he could possibly be violent if the occasion arose."

Davis Police Detective Fred Turner knew that if Hunt committed the Riggins-Gonsalves murders, Thompson likely knew about it, perhaps even participated. Thompson and wife Valerie were named on the witness section on the marriage license at David and Suellen Hunt's wedding in Carson City

— a wedding held the same day that John and Sabrina were abducted a three-hour drive away in Davis.

Still on the lam for escaping from San Quentin less than a month before, Thompson used an alias when signing the witness section of Hunt's 1980 marriage license — Richard Schneider. Turner traced this name to an Arizona driver's license that in turn led to Thompson.

In 1987, Turner learned, Thompson was on parole and scraping by in the Cecil Hotel in Los Angeles, an old hotel in one of downtown L.A.'s seediest sections. In July, Turner, Biondi, Sacramento Sheriff's Detective Bob Bell and Lopez flew from Sacramento to Los Angeles.

They hatched a plan to get Thompson to talk about the Davis killings. Wired with a voice-activated tape recorder that he wore in a shoulder holster under a sweatshirt, Lopez would buddy up to Thompson in the Cecil and tell him that he had recently talked to David Hunt, and that Hunt, facing 35 years of federal prison time, wanted Thompson to break him out of the Lompoc federal pen. It would be a quid pro quo for the time Hunt broke Thompson out of San Quentin seven years prior.

On July 14, 1987, Lopez, wearing the hidden recorder, knocked on Thompson's door on the 11th floor of the rickety hotel. Lopez told Thompson he found his address through a friend at the Department of Motor Vehicles. While Thompson was excited by the prison-breakout ruse, Lopez's attempt to get a full confession on tape was marred by series of blunders.

"Before we let Ray go in and wired him up to talk to Thompson, we had a long talk with him in downtown L.A.," Biondi remembered. "We told him, 'If it's not on tape, it doesn't count. I don't care what you think he says, if it's not on the audiotape, it does not count. And don't push for details. Just establish a rapport and then we'll come back.'"

Recalling this, Biondi shook his head.

"Having said all that, Ray did all the wrong things."

Anxious to get a confession, Lopez ignored the advice to go slow. He pressed Thompson about the murders from the start. After talking to Thompson in his room, the two headed down to the hotel bar, where they swilled beer and tequila, though Lopez claimed he remained sober. It is here that Lopez maintained he got a full confession out of Thompson. Based on this conversation with Thompson, the informant made the following statement to Fred Turner:

"After having a few drinks with Thompson, Thompson asked how I knew that they killed Riggins and Gonsalves, when there were only three people that knew, and that was David Hunt, Richard Thompson, and David Hunt's wife, Suellen," Lopez said. "And I indicated that I had been visiting with David, and that's how I knew.

"After talking with him for a while and drinking beers with him, Thompson admitted that it was David Hunt's idea to kill the kids, because his brother, Gerald Gallego, was incarcerated at that time for several murders, and he was going to do a copycat murder so it will take the heat off his brother.

"Thompson indicated that David Hunt was the one that killed John Riggins, and also that John Riggins gave him some sort of problems physically, so David Hunt had to calm him down.

"Richard Thompson also stated that he was the one that killed Gonsalves, that she was pleading with him not to kill her, and he stated to her that he wasn't going to kill her and says: Everybody does that before they get killed. And while talking to him a little longer and having a few drinks with him, (Thompson) indicated how David Hunt broke him out of San Quentin. He said that David Hunt put some sort of charcoal and polish, or some sort of chemical substance, or something on his skin to make him look darker. And that the wig he was wearing at the time of the escape was given to David Hunt by Thompson's old lady.

"From there they went on a nine-state crime spree, robbery spree, rather. And that at some point — in Arizona, I believe — they were going to buy some property, a restaurant and bar. But they didn't make it. They were arrested.

"And (Thompson) stated that Suellen, David Hunt's wife, was squeamish about the murders and that he doesn't trust her, and if given the word he will kill her because she could be a witness to murder."

This is what Ray Lopez told authorities he heard. What he actually got on tape is another thing entirely. If Thompson confessed in the bar, it is inaudible, drowned out by bar noise, including a loud jukebox. There is plenty of dialogue on other tapes at other times and locations between Thompson and Lopez, most of it rambling on topics unrelated to the murders. Thompson does come across as a bit racist and foul-mouthed — much of what he talks about is profanity-laced boasting of his sexual conquests — but there is little if anything specifically incriminating about the killings.

There is, however, one bit of dialogue caught on tape that, depending on how one interprets it — certainly in how Turner interpreted it — implicates Thompson and David Hunt. During a subsequent visit to Thompson's room,

Lopez brings up the killings, and starts out talking about Suellen's role. According to court transcripts of this recorded conversation (I have copies of the tapes and, like many who have listened to them, found them mostly inaudible), the alleged incriminating dialogue goes as follows:

Lopez: "David's main concern is that killing in Davis. That's his main concern."

Thompson: "What?"

Lopez: "The killing."

Thompson: "Yeah."

Lopez: "That's what he is concerned about. You know, he's worried about, you know, her being a witness."

Thompson: "Yeah. Hold on. That's her decision. You know...other than, uh, there ain't no problem."

Lopez: "Yeah, but she could be a witness."

Thompson: "Well she can be, that all depends on what Dave says and how he wants it handled. You know? And, uh, have no doubt, that it has to be handled anyway, and he needs to make what he feels is the right decision, and he won't be afraid to make the right decision."

In his continuing quest to squeeze a confession out of Thompson on tape, Lopez at this point fabricates a story that he wants to hurt someone in Sacramento who wronged him and wants to "pay that person back."

Thompson mentions "kidnapping the motherfucker" as a possibility.

Lopez: "Kidnap him?"

Thompson: "Torture him, injure him, do whatever you want to..."

Lopez: "What are you going to tie him up with?"

Thompson: "Who gives a fuck?"

Lopez: "What's the best thing to do it with?"

Thompson: "I don't know, carry handcuffs?"

Lopez: "No, not handcuffs. I know you've killed people before...I want him to suffer, you know what I mean? I want him to suffer, I want him to see...I'm talking about tying him up or whatever. What do I use?"

Thompson: "You can use whatever you want to, I mean..."

Lopez: "What's the best thing."

Thompson: "Whatever is handiest."

Lopez: "Well, what did you and Dave use?"

Thompson: "I got to (inaudible), you know, a piece of rope."

Lopez: "Come on now, don't bullshit, man. You know, I mean, what's a good thing to use?"

Thompson: "A whole lot of motherfucking tape."

Lopez: "Tape?"

Thompson: "Uh-huh. I'm going to duct tape the son of a bitch."

Lopez: "Duct tape? Does it work good enough?"

Thompson: "It does. You put duct tape around your wrists, you ain't going to get out of it."

Lopez: "How would you do it, from the front, or to the back?"

Thompson: "The only way to do it, you do it from the back...for safety purposes. I'm very safety conscious."

The conversation continues, but Lopez never gets anything more incriminating than the "duct tape" comment. In fact, Thompson — who reportedly had poor hearing and may very well have misunderstood Lopez in the noisy bar — at one point suggests fishing line may even be better for binding victims as it does not pick up fingerprints.

It is the most incriminating thing Lopez got on tape (though Thompson also mentions he liked to rob Lucky stores because he was familiar with their layout). Incriminating, Turner believed, because Sabrina and John were bound with duct tape, a detail that was never made public.

Thompson, police said, fled the hotel after he became suspicious of Lopez while doing both his and Lopez's laundry and finding a phone number marked for the Los Angeles Police Department in Lopez's pants pocket.

The next time the two men would see each other would be in court.

Joel Davis

92

snitch

17
Suellen
- - - - - - - - - - - - - - - - - -

"You mean to tell me I've been celebrating (my wedding anniversary)
on the wrong day all these years?"

— Suellen Hunt

U nlike the other initial suspects in the Riggins-Gonsalves murders, Suellen
Hunt grew up in a loving, middle-class family, earned a college degree,
attended law school, and had neither a history of drug abuse nor a criminal
record. At first glance, she appears to have more in common with John and
Sabrina than the people she was suspected of helping to kill them.

Born in 1944, the former Suellen Mae Shirley is the second of two daughters raised by attentive parents. The family lived in an upscale, two-story
Bay Area neighborhood in a home that Suellen lives in to this day taking
care of her elderly mother. Her late father, Howard Shirley, was a clerk for a
longshoreman's union. He doted on Suellen's mother, who was first a home-
maker and later a successful real estate agent in the East Bay Area. "Dad put
mom on a pedestal," Suellen recalled.

Thin and attractive with wavy brown hair, Suellen is no dummy. In the
early 1960s she was accepted into the University of the Pacific in Stockton,
a prestigious private school that put Suellen on academic probation and for
a time kicked her out. She eventually returned to get a B.A. in 1971. In the
late 1960s, she went through a hippie stage, even lived in a commune in the
early 1970s. It was also in the late '60s that Suellen married Mark Brifman,
an attorney. The two had a daughter, Leah, in 1969, and she would be a witness in this case. (Citing her young age at the time, Leah more often than
not answered "I don't remember" when asked key questions about the weekend of the murders.)

While married to Brifman, Suellen attended law school for a year. Suellen
and Brifman divorced in 1971. In 1973, Suellen married Bill Banner,* a then-

David and Suellen Hunt and Suellen's daughter Leah.

hippie who at one time allegedly helped Hunt grow marijuana in the master bedroom of a Menlo Park, Calif., home he owned with Suellen.

When Suellen and David Hunt were married on Dec. 20, 1980, she was still married to Banner. Her interests were in psychology, specifically psychodrama, a method for helping people become more creative in day-to-day living. In 1978, Suellen was hired as a rehabilitation counselor in the mental health department of the Santa Clara County Jail.

Here she began her love affair with career criminal David Hunt, in jail for stealing sheets from a San Jose Holiday Inn to sell for drug money. Although an educated, attractive woman from a middle-class family would seem an unlikely pairing with an uneducated bad-ass whose nefarious pedigree included a half-brother who would become a serial killer, Suellen fell hard and fast for the muscular, macho Hunt, perhaps, some say, because she felt she could "save" him.

(When I asked Suellen how she could fall for a career criminal with no apparent job skills or assets, she got defensive and said only, "There are a lot of people who really like David and respect him.")

She seemed willing to do anything for him, including smuggling drugs into prison for Hunt to both ingest and deal. Her relationship with him led to her firing as a jail counselor in 1979.

When Fred Turner in 1987 learned of Suellen's wedding to Hunt in Carson City on the day of John and Sabrina's abduction/murder, he focused on her. Suellen, Turner discovered, worked at a title company and lived in Arroyo Grande, about 60 miles from Lompoc, where her husband was locked up for the 1985 knifepoint kidnapping of a young Washington couple.

Though police informant Ray Lopez claimed he got Thompson to confess to the killings, there was nothing recorded more damning than Thompson's "duct tape" comment in describing how to restrain a kidnap victim.

Wanting something more incriminating, veteran Sacramento homicide supervisor Lt. Ray Biondi had another undercover job for Lopez: Go to Suellen's home and get something on tape. On July 21, 1987, Lopez, fresh from his L.A. visit with Richard Thompson, took a bus to Arroyo Grande, again concealing a wire under his clothes as he knocked on Suellen's door. He told her that he had recently talked with Richard Thompson.

"Richard Thompson thinks you're going to squeal to authorities about the Davis slayings," Lopez told Suellen. "If he gets a chance, he's going to take you out."

Suellen thought there was something familiar about Lopez — that she may have met him once at a party, or some such — but she said she did not really recognize this odd little man on her doorstep telling her her life was in danger.

"I guess I was supposed to know who he was when he showed up to the door," Suellen recalled. "All I could do was be terrified." And suspicious. "David had been very careful since he was in prison to keep anybody separate from me," she noted. "And certainly he would not have given my address to anybody. All of a sudden this man who didn't look very reputable was at my door."

Though frightened by Lopez's visit and what he told her, Suellen did not say anything incriminating. She told Lopez that on about Dec. 18 or 19, 1980, she drove a rental van from Menlo Park to meet David "out of state" and was accompanied by her daughter and several pets. As for the murders, Suellen told Lopez, "I don't know if (Thompson) did them or not."

Biondi shook his head when recalling the ruse.

"My idea backfired, just scared the crap out of the poor lady," he said, bluntly.

Cops generally have a lot of leeway with the law when it comes to lying in order to snare suspected criminals. They can fabricate who they are, what they're doing and why they're doing it. They can falsify documents, even secure bogus driver's licenses from the DMV. But trying to trick Suellen into a confession by telling her her life was in danger pushed the envelope.

"It's not really something that law enforcement ought to have been involved in doing," maintained Bob Bell, then a Sacramento homicide detective who worked the case with Biondi and Turner. "At the time it seemed like an appropriate way to see if there was any validity as to what was going on. I wouldn't say it backfired, it just didn't develop any information."

Actually, some incidental information was developed, and it was startling: It was around this time that the investigators learned that informant Ray Lopez was David Hunt's former brother-in-law, something Lopez did not bother to reveal when he first approached Biondi with his belief that Hunt killed the Davis couple.

Hunt and Gloria Lopez* wed in 1963, had two children, and divorced in 1972 during one of Hunt's many prison stints. Depending on how you look at it, Ray Lopez's relation to Hunt either worsened or boosted his credibility: Worsened because Hunt was, by all appearances, a negligent husband and Lopez may have wanted to make Hunt pay for how he treated Gloria. On the other hand, Lopez knew Hunt and Gallego better than most, knew of their fierce loyalty — and pieced together the copycat theory before anybody else.

Rattled by the Lopez visit, Suellen phoned the Sacramento County Sheriff's Department. She was referred to Turner, who, despite being in on Biondi's plan, claimed to know nothing. Friends and family who had been contacted by a determined Turner seeking details that might link Suellen to the slayings, soon alerted Suellen.

Suellen again phoned Turner. This time the Davis detective admitted investigating the case. But he was untruthful with Suellen, telling her that in L.A. Lopez had surreptitiously recorded Thompson saying he wanted Suellen dead. Wanting more information, Turner and Bell contacted Thompson's wife, Valerie. Valerie worried about being arrested for helping Hunt break her husband out of prison seven years prior. "Don't worry about the escape," the detectives told Valerie. "We want to know what you recall about the Hunt wedding on Dec. 20, 1980."

Valerie revealed that in the days prior to the wedding, she, Hunt and Thompson lived in some rundown apartments in a Phoenix barrio. On Dec. 18, the night before the three of them drove to Carson City, Thompson and Hunt engaged in what she characterized as a bizarre blood brother ritual where they seemed to make a pact of sorts.

Valerie later added that on the day of the wedding, Suellen drove from her Menlo Park home in a rental van to meet Hunt. She said that there was no celebration after the wedding and that the group returned to the Phoenix apartments.

In late July 1987, Turner and Suellen again talked by phone. Suellen denied any involvement in the murders. "I would know if I was in Davis, California, and I wasn't," she maintained. "And if I was in Davis, California, I would have packed up and left when I heard that this Mr. Thompson was going to kill me over it…I wouldn't have called you guys and asked you to check out Lopez…Everybody who has ever known me will tell you I would not sit by and watch a couple of kids my daughter's age get murdered."

After some back and forth with the investigators over dates and times relevant to the murders, Suellen — whom Turner has called a "master of doublespeak" — got frustrated as the conversation wore on and said, "I feel like I'm in the 'Twilight Zone.'"

On Aug. 4, Turner and Detective Bell took Valerie Thompson to Carson City to find the Motel 6 the wedding party checked into. Valerie identified the motel along with Bell's wedding chapel as the wedding site. She also recalled that a third person made the trip from Phoenix, a muscular blond man about 22 years old who knew Hunt from the Phoenix apartments and revered his outlaw lifestyle.

On Aug. 12, Suellen agreed to talk to Turner and Bell in person. Using the Arroyo Grande Police Station interrogation room, Turner and Bell peppered her with questions. Suellen conceded she was still married to Banner when she married Hunt in 1980. At the time, Hunt was wanted for breaking Thompson out of San Quentin, and Suellen said the reason they got married was for spousal immunity so she would not have to testify against Hunt for the escape. (A flawed plan, however, because marriage *after* a crime does not provide spousal immunity.)

"We figured that it was very unlikely the authorities were going to bother to go to all the trouble to find out where I got divorced and when and such, and, therefore, wouldn't make me testify against him and all of that," Suellen told the two detectives.

As the interview continued, Suellen also gave the wrong date and location of the wedding. She originally said she and Hunt were married on Dec. 19, 1980, in Las Vegas. (Suellen also gave this date and location to authorities as early as 1985 when Hunt was sentenced for the Washington kidnapping. So if she forgot the location/date of her nuptials, she forgot within five years of the wedding.)

She also said that following the afternoon ceremony, the wedding party drove back to Phoenix because they did not want to spend the money for another night at the Motel 6. Turner, who had a copy of the wedding certificate from Dec. 20, 1980, in Carson City, showed it to Suellen. Her nervous response darkened the cloud of suspicion over her head:

"Very seriously? And that's where I got married?" she replied. "You mean to tell me I've been celebrating on the wrong day all these years?"

After conceding that she and Hunt did indeed get married on Dec. 20 in a sleepy northern Nevada city a mere three hours from Davis as opposed to bustling, bright Las Vegas, an 11-hour drive from Davis in southern Nevada, Suellen claimed an ignorance of geography that she said is shared by Hunt.

"I don't know how close Las Vegas is to Carson City."

"A long way," Turner countered.

"I don't mean to be acting stupid. I really, really — and David thought it was — we both thought it was Las Vegas. I asked him where we got married."

Turner's skepticism grew. Now Suellen's rental van the weekend of the wedding was of great interest. Particularly the mileage on the rental contract.

Witnesses at the Lucky shopping center in Davis reported seeing vans in the parking lot the night of John and Sabrina's abduction. The descriptions of the vans are sketchy and inconsistent; one may or may not have been the Riggins Chevy van.

Because Suellen rented a van in Palo Alto that weekend to drive her daughter, her belongings and her pets to Carson City to meet up with and marry David Hunt, Turner speculated that one of the vans seen near Lucky was Suellen's rental van being used as the "trailer" vehicle behind the Riggins van once the sweethearts were abducted. It would be the group's ride back to Carson City after the Riggins van was abandoned.

If he could find the rental contract, Turner figured, the recorded mileage would add to his case against Suellen. "We thought the mileage on the van was Palo Alto to Carson City, then to Davis, then (the murder scene), then back to Carson City," Turner said.

Turner also believed the time Suellen returned the van would show if there was time for it to be used in the murders. Turner needed to find the rental agency. He did — a year too late.

He spent countless hours grilling Suellen and others about where the van came from, and when and where it was returned. Ultimately Turner deduced from witness interviews in 1988 that the van was rented from a Hertz in Palo Alto and returned to a Hertz drop-off at an airport in Truckee. But by the time Turner learned this, Hertz had destroyed the records from 1980.

Turner maintained that Suellen deceived him about the rental, that she purposely lied and said it was from a Budget Rent a Car rather than a Hertz location. Court records show that Suellen found a receipt for a Budget rental on Dec. 10, 1980, that she gave to Turner during a search of her home in 1987.

"She knew when I first contacted her where she rented the van," Turner said. "She knew where it had been returned. She wanted to lead me down the road to Budget. If we had been able to pursue the right course when we first got to her in 1987, we would have found the rental contract. But by 1988 it was gone."

While Turner did not find the car rental receipt in searching Suellen's home, he did find something even more compelling: a $1,000 check Suellen made out to Doug Lainer the day before the Davis murders.

Lainer, a truck driver and one-time petty thief from Alameda County who struggled with heroin addiction, served time with David Hunt in San Quentin and had been paroled five days before the murders. Thin, fair-skinned and highly excitable, Lainer was on parole for his role in a pathetic robbery caper with Hunt. On Oct. 16, 1978, an off-duty police officer at a San Jose Holiday Inn noticed a broken lock on the storage room. The officer spotted Hunt and Lainer lurking around the area, and arrested the two after he saw the wiry Lainer bolting from the storage room with a bundle of 105 king-sized sheets worth $1,166. Because the two had criminal records, they were sentenced to San Quentin. Hunt was paroled on Oct. 14, 1980, Lainer on Dec. 15, 1980, four days before Suellen gave him the $1,000 check.

Asked by Turner in 1987 about the check from the Hunts, Lainer replied cryptically, "I don't know, you'll have to ask them."

Hunt declined to talk to authorities on the matter. But Suellen told Turner that "David wanted Doug to have it" and "they had been friends, Doug helped David out once, so David wanted to help Doug."

Turner started keeping close tabs on Doug Lainer.

Joel Davis

Suellen

18
Odyssey

Detective Fred Turner did not believe Suellen Hunt for a minute when she claimed to be confused about the time and place of her 1980 wedding to David Hunt. After all, he thought, who forgets when and where — especially *where* — they were married?

Turner also didn't buy Suellen's assertion that she married Hunt for spousal immunity to avoid being a witness in the November 1980 San Quentin escape. "Sue knew the escape was past the statute of limitations," Turner said. "We made it exceedingly clear what crime we were interested in."

While his Sacramento detective counterparts ultimately felt they didn't have much in the way of damning evidence against Suellen, her husband, or Richard Thompson, Turner forged ahead with tenacity. He had the blessing of Davis Police Chief Vic Mentink, who, nearing retirement and with children who went to school with John Riggins, wanted the case cleared.

After hounding Suellen in August 1987, Turner took off on a 5,000-mile odyssey interviewing friends, relatives and associates of the suspects in California, Arizona, Utah, Colorado, Washington and Montana. In all, he secured some two-dozen search warrants through affidavits while running up a considerable expense tab.

On Sept.15, 1987, Turner interrogated a cooperative Richard Thompson at the Santa Monica Police Department. He denied involvement with the murders and voluntarily gave his fingerprints. He took a polygraph exam, and, according to Turner, flunked all relevant questions except one that asked if he personally cut the victims' throats.

Three days later, detectives from the Sacramento County Sheriff's Department traveled to Lompoc Federal Prison to give a lie detector test to David Hunt — and found him in mid-visit with Suellen. The detective who tested Hunt said Hunt was not deceptive. The detectives then administered a polygraph examination to Suellen and concluded that she, too, was not being deceptive.

Fingerprints were taken from Hunt, Thompson and Suellen and compared to the 64 fingerprints found in the Riggins van. None matched.

Also in the fall of 1987, Gerald Gallego's ex-mother-in-law, Mercedes Williams, recalled for Turner that Hunt phoned her in November 1980 while Gallego was sought for the murders of Craig Miller and Mary Beth Sowers and asked if "there was anything, anything at all" that he could do.

Turner then talked to Gallego's wife, Charlene, by now in prison for her role in Gallego's sex-slave murders on a reduced sentence for testifying against her ex-husband. She said Gallego and Hunt were very tight and that Gallego sent her to San Quentin to visit Hunt twice in 1979.

Also in October, Turner contacted Bob and Audrey Reid, the couple who were spooked by two suspicious men walking out of a field not far from the murder scene the night of Dec. 20, 1980. He showed the Reids photographic lineups. These included two sets of six pictures each, one set with Hunt's picture and one with Thompson's. The Reids identified neither, though they did say the men they saw stood next to an older-model, light-colored van. (Turner believed this van to be the light-blue, 1966 Dodge van Hunt and Richard Thompson bought in Spokane, Wash., for $400 after Hunt broke him out of San Quentin. Hunt and Thompson drove the van from Phoenix to Carson City to meet Suellen.)

In November, Turner showed his photographic lineup to Kelly James, who told police that about 10 p.m. on the night of the slayings, she saw a suspicious-looking man walking along Folsom Boulevard near Rudy's Hideaway not far from the murder scene. In 1987, James said David Hunt most closely resembled the man she saw that night.

After interviewing James, Turner showed the lineup pictures to Joyce Hullender, the motorist who peeked into the Riggins van after she found it blocking part of Folsom Boulevard the night of the abduction. When Hullender was first interviewed on Dec. 23, 1980, she did not mention seeing anyone near the van, only that she was frightened by footsteps on the pavement. But after further reflection, she told Turner, she recalled a white man with a prominent nose entered the van as she peered inside it long enough to see crumpled wrapping paper strewn about and a pair of gloves and a red baseball hat in the driver's seat.

Hullender said that while she wished she had side views of the men in the pictures, she identified David Hunt's photo after saying, "If you force me to pick one, I'd say it's this one."

In early December 1987, Turner interviewed Rebecca Romani, the Davis woman and former schoolmate of John Riggins who, on the night of the abduction, was at the Lucky shopping center in Davis and saw two scruffy, thin, "unhealthy-looking" men in a breezeway while her family picked up a pizza. When she first talked to police in 1980, she described the men as white males between 18 and 23 years old.

Like the others, Romani failed to pick Thompson out of the photo lineup. But she noted that while the men she saw looked younger than the men in Turner's pictures, she identified Hunt — 36 at the time of the crime — as the one who most resembled the men she saw.

Turner also interviewed the restaurant cook who claimed to see John and Sabrina smiling at the menus outside the Chandelier restaurant at the shopping center. Like Romani, the cook noticed two suspicious men lurking about the shopping center that night, but did not identify Hunt or Thompson in the photo lineups.

In April 1988, Turner met with a longtime girlfriend of Thompson's, Diana Sherman. She said she was convinced that Thompson was guilty because Thompson told her following his interview with Turner he was positive his fingerprints would not be in Riggins' van because he "never took his gloves off." She added that Thompson liked to tie people up to control them and tie wrist and ankles to a garrote around his victims' necks so that movement induces choking. Turner found this significant because John and Sabrina had possible ligature (rope) marks on their necks, according to their autopsies.

Valerie Thompson told Turner that Suellen's rental van was returned in the Carson City area. On the return trip to Phoenix following the wedding, Valerie explained to Turner that she, Thompson, Hunt, Suellen and her daughter, the scruffy young blond man, and Suellen's pets all crowded into Thompson's blue Dodge van.

Turner badly wanted to find the young, blond wannabe outlaw who tagged along with Hunt and the Thompsons to the Carson City wedding. After considerable digging around, Turner learned the man's name was Bill Lansing. Turner found Lansing at a train station in Glasgow, Mont., on Sept. 27, 1988.

Turner took Lansing to the Carson City Motel 6 to refresh Lansing's admittedly fuzzy memory of the events of Dec. 20, 1980. While hazy on specifics, Lansing said that he and the Thompsons and Hunt left their seedy apartment complex in Phoenix shortly before sundown on Dec. 19 and arrived in Carson City about 7 a.m. on Dec. 20. Hunt, Lansing said, wore a disguise of a fake beard, colored hair and a cowboy hat when he got to Carson City, and hid a pearl-handled straight razor in his boot.

Lansing recalled that he and the rest of the Phoenix group met Suellen at the Motel 6 and then went out for breakfast. After the afternoon wedding, the group headed to the Carson City Nugget casino, where Lansing was left alone after Hunt told him, "We have family business to take care of."

Lansing said he was by himself for up to four hours, during which time he got drunk at the casino. His next clear memory, he told Turner, was waking up in one of two rooms the wedding party had at the Motel 6. He had no recollection of who did what overnight, nor did he recall who drove him from the casino back to the motel. On the drive back to Phoenix on Dec. 21, Lansing said the mood in the crowded van was somber.

Turner had believed for some time that the Hunt party had a motive for the Riggins-Gonsalves slayings — a Hunt-conceived copycat killing to take the heat off Gallego. Now his conversations with Lansing confirmed his suspicions that the group had the opportunity to kill the young sweethearts.

It was time to close the ring.

19
Busted

HEARTY CONGRATULATIONS TO ALL

"The families and friends of John Riggins and Sabrina Gonsalves are understandably grateful for the efforts of the Davis police in building a case against those suspected of killing the teen-agers...In particular, praise is being directed toward Davis Police Detective Fred Turner...This sends a message that crime in Davis simply will not be tolerated and that police will not give up, no matter how long it takes to solve a crime."

— Davis Enterprise editorial
Nov. 14, 1989

By early 1989, Fred Turner had been regularly updating Yolo County District Attorney David Henderson on the Riggins-Gonsalves case. Henderson, a law-and-order conservative, had been district attorney since 1984, when he beat Davis liberal Bob Black for the post. He was a young deputy district attorney in Davis when John and Sabrina were killed.

"I followed the case from its outset," Henderson, a football star in college, said in his trademark low monotone, earning him the nickname "Mumbles" in some circles. "In fact, I went out to the body-recovery area at the time. You really can't get an idea of what the setting is like unless you see it."

Henderson was impressed enough with Turner's burgeoning case against the "Hunt group" that in February 1989 he assigned one of his office's own veteran investigators, John Haynes, 55, to help Turner close in on an arrest. Haynes, a respected detective and something of an eccentric, got his start with the Sacramento County Sheriff's Department.

Squeezed into a broom closet-sized room, the two detectives focused on David and Suellen Hunt and the man Hunt broke out of prison a month before John and Sabrina were killed, Richard Thompson. They also started questioning Doug Lainer, who did time with Hunt and Thompson in

David Henderson
Davis Enterprise

San Quentin and was given the $1,000 check by Suellen the day before the slayings.

Haynes familiarized himself with Turner's investigation. He decided there was something to Turner's theory on Hunt and his associates.

"After I felt OK with the basic thrust, Fred and I began a sorting process of all identifiable items – physical evidence, crime scene information, photos, statements," Haynes said. The two had interns and civilian helpers process each page of each report in the massive case. They then did what Haynes called a "written triage," giving each category an identification code and entering it into a computer program. This took several months, during which the two detectives met with Henderson several times. They were sure they had the right suspects.

As Yolo County's interest in the case grew, Sacramento County's interest waned. The more Turner, Haynes and Henderson seemed to subscribe to the Hunt theory, the less Sacramento Sheriff's Lt. Ray Biondi and his charges seemed to agree. While Turner and Haynes were convinced that their witnesses were credible, their counterparts in Sacramento had doubts.

Biondi, the person who originally told Turner of the Hunt theory, began getting cold feet, though he remained nominally supportive of Yolo's efforts, especially in the press. He didn't like the quality of the tapes from the Ray Lopez/Richard Thompson undercover operation, and he didn't like the so-called eyewitness accounts that implicated the Hunt group. "I'm bothered by the fact that I don't see any credible evidence that we could put (the suspects) in California regardless of what all these witnesses say," Biondi said in 2001. "At one point I was convinced that they were responsible. The thing that bothered me is we cannot put them in the area of the murders, cannot put them in California."

Biondi also doubted whether John and Sabrina were in fact abducted at the Lucky shopping center as opposed to Sabrina's condo. A condo abduction suggests a stalker who knew the victims rather than someone seeking a couple at random for a copycat killing.

"The condo seemed more logical in that it was nearly deserted at the Christmas holiday," Biondi observed. "What bothered me about the shopping center is there were people who saw (John and Sabrina) looking at the menus in the windows and all of that. Well, they were late in getting to the sister's birthday party. It doesn't seem like they would be lollygagging around the shopping center."

Biondi and his two primary detectives who worked the case, Bob Bell and Stan Reed, also were alarmed by Turner's police reports chronicling Lopez's attempts to tape record damning statements by Thompson and Suellen.

"We could listen to the same tape, write two separate reports, and (Turner's) report doesn't comport with what I was writing. So that's a problem," said Bell, famed for his detective work leading to the arrests of Symbionese Liberation Army members in connection with the 1975 slaying of Myrna Opsahl at Crocker National Bank in Carmichael.

And while Turner was convinced that Suellen lied during her interrogations, Bell wasn't so sure.

"We sat her down for a long time," Bell remembered. "She just denied any knowledge of what was going on in Sacramento. And it never got any closer than that. I walked out of there going maybe yes, maybe no. I didn't walk out of there thinking these are the right people. I walked out of there going well, I'm not sure."

Another thing that bothered Bell was that informant Lopez's alleged confession from Richard Thompson depicted a scenario in which Valerie Thompson took part in the blood ritual, accompanied the wedding party to Carson City — yet knew nothing of the murder conspiracy.

Biondi said that Turner did some good detective work, including tracking down David Hunt in 1987 when Biondi's force could not. But Biondi, like many, believed the Davis detective lost his objectivity along the way. Biondi was especially alarmed when he compared Turner's reports to Bell's after both men monitored Lopez's attempts to record Thompson in L.A. "When we saw Fred's report, we were astounded," Biondi recalled. "What was there is not what was said."

In fact, in his sworn affidavits seeking search warrants for Suellen's home, Turner wrote that Lopez recorded Thompson confessing — rather than saying what really happened, that Lopez said he recorded a confession that was drowned out by a bar jukebox.

Turner ultimately corrected the discrepancy in later warrants, but not before Yolo County Municipal Court Judge Donna Petre approved the originals containing the inaccuracies. Turner, in essence, searched Suellen's home on the strength of inaccurate information he swore was true when he submitted it. The originals were never corrected. "We never went back to the pages and rewrote them because (Petre) would read the new pages. She already knew what the old pages said," Turner said.

As Biondi and his charges in Sacramento grew wary of Turner's investigation, Turner and others in Davis and Yolo County law enforcement began wondering why Sacramento County homicide investigators, Stan Reed in particular, didn't chase the Hunt lead more vigorously when tips about it surfaced as early as four days after the murders.

Reed had talked to Hunt in person in March 1981 and on the phone in April 1982. The first time Hunt declined to talk because he said he was on parole. The second time, he told Reed he was in Phoenix the day of the murders. "Reed could have squeezed him harder," Turner said, adding that taking Hunt's word for it over the phone was inadequate given Hunt's record as a career criminal. "That's all he did. Did he go to Phoenix to talk to him in person? No."

Hunt was under no legal obligation to talk to Reed, and Reed said he could only do so much. "He wouldn't talk to us," Reed noted. "What were we going to do? Beat him down with a stick?"

Turner also believed Biondi, who devoted a significant amount of time and manpower to chasing down Gallego in the 1980s — and even wrote a book about it in 1987 — didn't want to jeopardize the Gallego case by involving Charlene Gallego in the Riggins-Gonsalves case. "It was political, (Biondi) didn't want to give her a chance for changing the story. They didn't want to lose Gerry Gallego."

Despite Biondi's doubts, Turner and Haynes pressed ahead with the investigation of a case that ironically had been initiated by the very homicide unit that now doubted its veracity. Although now living in Atlanta, John Riggins' mother, Kate, kept in regular touch with Biondi and Reed during this time and grew to trust and admire both detectives. Biondi and Reed drove to San Francisco and met with Kate and Dr. Riggins at an orthopedic surgeons conference. "Yolo is probably going to arrest them," Biondi told them. "But I'm here to warn you that it's my opinion that the case is not going to result in a conviction."

Biondi also took part in a heated summer 1989 meeting between Sacramento District Attorney John Dougherty, Deputy District Attorney John O'Mara, Yolo DA Henderson and others. O'Mara, a very careful and skeptical prosecutor, pored over the case, listened to the Thompson tapes, found them mostly useless, decided there wasn't enough evidence, and opted not to prosecute it despite Henderson strongly urging him to do so.

"There were certainly things that pointed in (the suspects') direction and other things that were troublesome," recalled O'Mara, who felt pressured by Henderson while feeling that Biondi and his investigators were too sidetracked by other cases to discredit Turner's theories. "Putting that to the side, the quality of the evidence wasn't such that I felt we had a reasonable probability of securing a conviction."

Henderson, O'Mara said, "was sort of bullying us to do the right thing. I think he was trying to bully the sheriff's department and in turn bullying us."

O'Mara, Sacramento County's gatekeeper on murder cases, is a stickler for details who loves playing devil's advocate with beleaguered detectives and prosecutors before he decides to file charges on a case. (Detectives who worked this case have told me O'Mara's Socratic approach, while difficult, ultimately made them better investigators.) O'Mara didn't like the quality of the so-called confession tapes ("if they aren't clear to me, then 12 jurors won't get it"), and he was wary of informant Lopez. "Jurors have a healthy dose of skepticism when you offer a jailhouse informant or any kind of informant, and they rightfully should," he said. "Turner was another problem with the case. I think Fred, with the best of intentions, just got too close to this case and lost some objectivity."

Fortified by Turner and Haynes' findings, Henderson decided to go for it. "If you don't arrest them I will," he warned O'Mara. Like Turner and Haynes, Henderson believed the evidence clearly demonstrated that the Hunt group had the motive and the opportunity to kill John and Sabrina. "I felt that we were going to be able to present a sequence of circumstances that indicated their responsibility and that they were not going to be able to offer any alternative explanation," Henderson said.

Henderson prepared the no-bail arrest warrants for David Hunt, 45, his wife, Suellen, 45, and Richard Thompson, 51. On Nov. 7, Haynes and Turner presented the warrants to Yolo County Municipal Court Judge Doris Shockley, who signed all three. Each warrant charged two counts of first-degree murder with special circumstances. If convicted, the suspects faced the death penalty.

Prior to his arrest for the murders, Thompson, now in the California Institute for Men in Chino for yet another parole violation, was offered a plea bargain by Henderson of two concurrent 25-years-to-life sentences and no death penalty in exchange for testifying against suspected mastermind David Hunt. He declined.

The day after securing the arrest warrants, Turner and Haynes flew to Pennsylvania to arrest Hunt and Suellen. Hunt, serving 35 years for the 1985 Washington state kidnapping, had been transferred from federal prison in Lompoc, Calif., to Lewisburg, Pa., because Suellen had smuggled drugs to him in Lompoc. Although not allowed to visit Hunt because of her role in the drug smuggling, Suellen dutifully followed her husband to Pennsylvania and rented a one-bedroom cabin in North Heidelberg Township. She had a good job and, she felt, a bright future.

On Nov. 9, the two detectives, accompanied by Pennsylvania state troopers in unmarked cars, descended on the cabin. A startled Suellen came out, and at first did not recognize Turner. Once she remembered Turner from their encounters in 1987, she allowed the detectives to search the cabin. Suellen was then taken to a nearby police station, where Turner pressed her for information, including the rental contract for the van she drove the weekend of the murders.

In a surreal moment, Turner told Suellen "You're facing the death penalty," then added, "Would you like a Pepsi?"

Suellen didn't respond, so Haynes asked, "Will you drink a Mountain Dew?"

Death penalty? Soft drink? Whaddya have?

Suellen still didn't respond. When Turner pressed her about giving the wrong day and location of her wedding to Hunt, she again claimed to have a confused memory and countered, "All I did was get (to Carson City), change my clothes and get married...And that's the truth. There is no way to convince you people...All I can do is hope the justice system works...I'm not about to say that I have done something that I haven't done."

Suellen also said that she believed they drove back to Phoenix the night of the 20th rather than staying the night at the Carson City Motel 6. She spent her wedding night in the Phoenix apartment because they did not want to stay another night and wanted to save the $40. Turner and Haynes then handcuffed Suellen, who waived extradition, and accompanied her on a flight to Sacramento.

Hunt and Thompson were arrested in prison. Thompson showed little emotion. Hunt, arrested in the warden's office of the federal prison in Lewisburg, clenched his jaw and leveled an icy stare at the two detectives as they finished reading him his rights. "Fuck you," he hissed, then returned to his cell. He was extradited to Sacramento under heavy guard on a federal marshal's jet used to transport dangerous prisoners.

Although the arrests were made on Nov. 9, Turner and Haynes convinced the judge at Suellen's Pennsylvania extradition hearing to impose a 30-day news blackout. The blackout lasted four days as rumors of an arrest in the most shocking crime in Davis history began to percolate.

On Monday, Nov. 13, 1989, the arrests of David and Suellen Hunt and Richard Thompson were made public. The arrests came almost nine years after John and Sabrina were slain. Despite the time gap, the arrests made national news, and were a lead story in Northern California newspapers and newscasts. The Davis Enterprise ran what to this day remains one of its largest front-page headlines since the newspaper was founded in 1898:

POLICE MAKE ARRESTS IN '80 DAVIS SLAYINGS

Given that the murders rocked both the university and the community at large, Davis residents were elated, relieved – and surprised that an arrest had actually been made in a case that seemed so dormant. Friends of John and Sabrina, now scattered all over the country starting families, finishing college, building careers – doing the things John and Sabrina never got a chance to do – called one another, saying, "You're not going to believe this..."

Fred Turner was a hero. Everyone from the media to the victims' families hailed his dogged detective work. He was seen as heroic as the suspects – two hardened cons and a femme fatale – were villainous. He began entertaining ideas of writing a book on the compelling case.

The Nov. 13, 1989, Davis Enterprise announcing the arrest of the Hunt group, left, and an ensuing story chronicling the dogged detective work of Yolo investigators Fred Turner (top) and John Haynes.

Henderson knew prosecuting the trio would be costly in cash-strapped Yolo County. Even before the arrests were announced, he made sure that the investigation and prosecution would be paid for from a special fund. He hoped that Thompson or Suellen would roll on Hunt — that plea agreements would reduce the number of suspects requiring lengthy court hearings and trials.

After all, Charlene Gallego had turned state's evidence against Gerald Gallego. Henderson figured that faced with the death penalty, either Thompson, Suellen or both would do the same thing against David Hunt — because it was Hunt he wanted most of all.

20
Hunt

When Davis residents learned of David Hunt's arrest as the suspected lead killer in the Riggins-Gonsalves case, it was as if Central Casting sent in the perfect bogeyman to finally provide a suspect and motive for the most notorious and puzzling crime in city history.

Hunt's frightening record of violent assaults and prison escapes, his close relationship with half-brother and notorious serial killer Gerald Gallego, his dubious ties to the Sacramento area, his muscular, tattooed body – all morphed into a personification of evil the likes of which had never been seen in Davis. Ground zero for that evil seemed to be David Hunt's obsidian gaze, a look as chilling as the fog that enveloped Davis on Dec. 20, 1980.

"The most telling thing about David Hunt are his eyes," maintained Fred Turner. "They're very cold and there is nothing there."

"He had a cold, icy stare," added Sabrina's brother, Stephen, who viewed Hunt in court.

David Hunt's empty eyes are the windows to a seemingly empty existence, a life marked by crime, drug abuse, failed relationships, psychiatric problems and a childhood as sad as John and Sabrina's was happy. Hunt and Gallego's mother, Lorraine, was married four times and had four sons. After a failed first marriage, she wed Hunt's father, Harold Hunt, in 1943. The two soon divorced – David Hunt, born in 1944, never knew his father. In 1945, Lorraine married Gerald Gallego Sr. Like the son he fathered in 1946, the senior Gallego was a murderer: He killed a town marshal in Ocean Springs, Miss., in the early 1950s and was executed in 1953. While in prison, the elder Gallego beat a jailer to death with a pipe after throwing cleaning acid in his eyes.

Lorraine Hunt's third husband, George Bulgar, was the man of the house during David and Gerald's youth. Bulgar, a bartender, treated David "very cruelly," court records show. At the same time, David's mother rejected him because she did not know how to control him. She also blamed him for corrupting his younger half-brother Gerald.

David Hunt in court following his arrest.

Davis Enterprise

With little if any parental affection or guidance, David and Gerald began depending on each other – and getting into trouble. Hunt dropped out of Rio Linda Junior High School in the eighth grade. In 1962, while he, Gallego and five other robbers held up a Sacramento bar called the Stumble Inn, he shot a patron who accosted him because the patron didn't believe Hunt's gun was real. Hunt and Gallego then robbed a Sacramento hotel, then a liquor store, ordering the clerk to get on the floor or they would shoot him.

In 1963, Hunt married Gloria Lopez, sister of Ray Lopez, the snitch who told police Hunt killed John and Sabrina. They had a boy and girl whom Hunt largely ignored: At the time of his arrest in 1989, Hunt had gone a decade without seeing them. A wife and kids did not slow Hunt down. He and Gallego continued to commit robberies and burglaries throughout the 1960s, along with dealing and taking drugs. In 1969, the duo attempted to rob a Vacaville motel. The police were alerted, and found Hunt pointing a .45-caliber pistol at the motel manager and his wife. When an officer ordered Hunt to drop the gun, he shot at the officer, but the pistol misfired. Gallego, meanwhile, had fled, and was found hiding in a nearby restaurant.

They were booked into Solano County Jail, where they escaped by sawing their way through a barred window. They were captured three weeks later in San Francisco. At trial, Hunt, 25, who as a teen was found to be emotionally disturbed, was declared insane, though at least one psychiatrist thought he was faking. Eight months after being admitted into a mental hospital, he was declared sane.

Subsequent psychiatric exams in the 1970s found Hunt to be "a sociopath, who developed a psychotic period based on overuse of (methamphetamine)." In 1976 Hunt claimed to hear voices in his head; a later evaluation found him to be a "paranoid schizophrenic as well as an antisocial personality."

Like his half-brother Gerald, Hunt's crimes seemed to get more violent as he got older. On Dec. 12, 1975, Hunt and another man and a woman were shooting pool at a Santa Clara County bar when Hunt suddenly grabbed the woman at knifepoint and twice tried to force her in a back room for reasons that aren't quite clear. The other man talked Hunt out of it, so he settled on robbing the woman and the bar's cash register. Not long after this, Hunt was arrested for robbing a Santa Clara drug store.

While Hunt likely got away with many crimes, like Thompson, he also got caught a lot, including the almost-comedic attempt with Doug Lainer to steal sheets from a Holiday Inn in 1978. This arrest landed Hunt in San Quentin from Jan. 1, 1979, to Oct. 14, 1980. As far as his suspected link to the Davis killings goes, this was an eventful incarceration: Hunt met and became romantically involved with Suellen, his intake counselor in jail before he went to prison, and where he became good friends with fellow prisoners Lainer and Richard Thompson.

Shortly after his release from San Quentin, Hunt resumed his life of violent crime, busting Thompson out of San Quentin on Nov. 24, 1980, and engaging in a multistate crime spree with Thompson before settling in the Phoenix apartment complex, which is where he claimed to be on Dec. 20, 1980. Hunt was arrested in February 1981 for helping Thompson escape. But he was never prosecuted because of problems with witnesses identifying the disguised Hunt, and lost evidence, including a photo lineup stolen from an officer's desk by a San Quentin inmate.

Hunt rarely had steady employment. The most stable job he appears to have had was a Bay Area house-cleaning business in the early 1980s, "G&D Cleaning" (possibly short for "Gerald and David"), which he told authorities he had to sell "because of Gerald's criminal situation."

Living off money Suellen got from selling her Menlo Park home, Hunt,

Suellen and Suellen's daughter, Leah, moved to Oregon in 1984. Hunt, long fascinated by firearms, gave Leah a .22-caliber pistol for Christmas 1980, when she was 11. In Oregon, Hunt listed his occupation as a woodcutter. But it was a front for growing and dealing marijuana under the alias Arthur McKay Durand.

A flap over a marijuana deal and some bad blood prompted Hunt and an accomplice to kidnap a young Tacoma, Wash., couple, Steven Skuza and Kirsten Baugher, on June 22, 1985, the so-called look-alike crime that led to Hunt's arrest in the Riggins-Gonsalves slayings. On this day, a female federal officer patrolling the Ft. Lewis military base near Tacoma spotted a green van in a wooded area at 1:15 a.m. The van was locked in for the night: The base closed at 6:30 p.m. and would not open again until 6 a.m.

The officer noticed Skuza on the floor of the van under a blanket; Baugher sat trembling next to him. Hunt and the van's driver, Timothy Langmeier, sat stoically up front. The officer asked for everyone's identification, then called for backup help when she noticed Skuza's limbs bound with white medical tape.

After backup help arrived, Langmeier surrendered, but Hunt bolted into the woods. A police dog tracked him down 20 minutes later. Found in the van were loaded firearms and knives. Skuza was severely beaten. Although she showed no signs of a physical assault and her clothes were not rumpled or dirty, Baugher said Hunt took her into the woods, removed her clothes, and raped her, but withdrew before ejaculating.

With little chance of beating the rap, Hunt made a plea agreement: In exchange for pleading guilty to kidnapping, he would not be prosecuted for the alleged rape. He was sentenced to 35 years in federal prison; he could have gotten life.

"Hunt has a long history of violent, assaultive behavior," wrote a probation officer who evaluated him for the sentencing judge. "Drug addiction and mental disorder have been the underlying theme of his various robberies and assault.

"It is noted in psychiatric reports going back to 1970 that he has wanted to work on his problems, seek counseling, and has openly taken responsibility for much of his criminal behavior.

"However, to date his criminal behavior continues. While his behavior has changed from holding up pharmacies, taverns and motel owners to assaulting and kidnapping drug dealers, the problem remains that the defendant apparently believes that he has the right to take the law into his own hands and use force, including weapons...Consistently through his criminal history clinicians have indicated that counseling is needed. Obviously it is — but for how long?"

A psychologist who tested and interviewed Hunt in 1985 said he had "low average intelligence," lacked problem-solving skills and tended to take action to solve problems rather than thinking them through.

"Mr. Hunt's conflicts with others and authorities stem from a strong preference for taking action now and asking questions later," the psychologist noted. The psychologist added, however, that Hunt was extremely loyal to family and thought of himself as a "protector and rescuer of others who were helpless and down-and-out."

Yolo County District Attorney David Henderson intended to prove that it was Hunt's fierce loyalty to Gerald Gallego that cost John and Sabrina their lives.

Joel Davis

118

Hunt

21
Prelim

G iven the Hunt party's history of prison escapes, security tightened for the trio's Yolo County arraignment and court appearances in 1989 and 1990. In a jarring contrast to Davis' tranquil milieu, sharpshooters crouched on roofs overlooking the tiny Davis Municipal Court, where preliminary hearings were held for the suspects, who were hustled to court in chains under heavy guard.

It was as if the Manson Family had invaded Mr. Rogers' Neighborhood.

There were two preliminary hearings in 1990. In California criminal cases, preliminary hearings determine whether there is sufficient evidence to go to trial. Unlike a criminal trial, which requires findings of guilt beyond a reasonable doubt, usually by a jury, preliminary hearings require a lesser standard — a strong suspicion of guilt by the judge hearing the case. They can be more interesting than a trial because they are usually more concise. "Prelims," as they are called, tend to be a forum for prosecutors to convince a judge that there is enough culpability to go forward with a trial. More often than not, defendants are bound over for trial.

Despite the administrative demands of his position, Yolo County District Attorney David Henderson opted to prosecute the Riggins-Gonsalves case himself. To save money and time, he tried combining the Hunts' and Richard Thompson's preliminary hearings. But David Hunt's legal team wasn't ready, so Suellen and Thompson's hearing was held first, in May 1990. Prior to the hearing, Henderson dropped the murder charges against Suellen and Thompson in a bit of legal razzle-dazzle designed to erase a set of judicial rulings he felt hurt his case, namely a ruling by Yolo County Municipal Court Judge William Lebov separating Hunt's case from the other two. Henderson refiled the charges a few days later. He also had Lebov removed from the case and replaced with Sacramento Municipal Court Judge Rudolph Loncke.

With no physical evidence, and eyewitness accounts eroded by the passage of almost a decade since the murders, Henderson's case relied heavily on a compelling sequence of events that he felt proved that the Hunt party had the motive and opportunity to kill John and Sabrina.

Henderson's central theory went as follows:

In the fall of 1980, David Hunt, Richard Thompson and Douglas Lainer were inmates at San Quentin, all in for robbery. Hunt was paroled Oct. 14.

With the help of his wife, Charlene, Gerald Gallego killed Sacramento State sweethearts Mary Beth Sowers and Craig Miller on Nov. 2 after kidnapping them at Arden Fair Mall. The Gallegos were arrested on the run in Nebraska on Nov. 17. Aware that his half-brother was on the lam and wanted for murder, David Hunt phoned Gallego's mother-in-law on Nov. 4 and asked her if there was anything he could do to help.

After the Gallegos' arrest, David Hunt set his copycat plan in motion by breaking Thompson out of San Quentin, even though Thompson only had about a year left on his sentence. Doug Lainer, Henderson maintained, took part in the escape by relaying information between Hunt and Thompson when he was allowed out of San Quentin for his mother's funeral on Nov. 20. Privy to the escape plans, Suellen recruited Thompson's wife, Valerie, to help with the Nov. 24 breakout.

After the escape and ensuing crime spree, the Thompsons and Hunt holed up in some low-rent apartments in Phoenix. On the morning of Dec. 19, Hunt and the Thompsons cut their wrists then rubbed them together in a blood ritual cementing their loyalty in a harbinger of the evil act to come. They then drove Hunt's van to Carson City to meet Suellen.

Meanwhile, back at her Bay Area home, Suellen on Dec. 19 gave Lainer — who was paroled from San Quentin on Dec. 15 — a $1,000 check to be a decoy in the murders. Henderson maintained she rented a van and drove her daughter, belongings and two dogs and up to seven cats to Carson City, where, on the morning of Dec. 20, she met Hunt and the Thompsons at a Motel 6.

That afternoon, Hunt and Suellen were wed between 1:30 and 2 p.m., with the Thompsons and William Lansing, the young tag-along from Phoenix, as witnesses. By marrying, Hunt and Suellen would have spousal immunity if they ever had to testify against one another for the heinous crime they were about to commit. After the wedding, Hunt informed Lansing they had "family business" and dropped him off at a casino in the late afternoon/early evening. They left Suellen's daughter and pets in a Carson City Motel 6 for the night with Valerie Thompson.

Driving one of the two vans at their disposal, Hunt, Thompson and Suellen hooked up with Lainer in the Sacramento area, most likely at the Rancho Cordova Motel 6, where a room may have been reserved (the motel records were checked but did not go back to 1980). They drove to Davis — a college town familiar to Suellen from her drive through Davis on her way to Carson City. Looking for a couple similar to Miller and Sowers to abduct at a shopping center, Henderson theorized, Hunt and Thompson noticed the attractive, well-dressed John and Sabrina at the Lucky parking lot, won their confidence, and then overpowered them in John's van.

Hunt and Thompson drove the van to Sacramento, where it was seen in several locations, including swerving on the Yolo Causeway. Hunt, known to have a poor sense of direction, possibly got lost in the fog along the way, which the Yolo investigators maintained accounted for all the van sightings at different Sacramento locations. Hunt and Thompson ultimately made their way to the ravine near Aerojet — which Hunt knew of from growing up in Sacramento — and killed the sweethearts. Although Sowers and Miller were shot to death, Henderson believed Hunt and Thompson resorted to using knives to kill John and Sabrina because a young couple on a date saw them in the area and they feared gunshots would draw attention.

Suellen and Lainer followed in one, maybe two, trailer vehicles, one of which provided transport for Suellen, Thompson and Hunt back to Carson City.

Like Miller and Sowers, the bodies were not buried or covered, and were dumped near the same road where Sowers' body was found. This and other similarities, Henderson believed, pointed to a copycat.

The group returned to Carson City sometime overnight. In the morning, they picked up Valerie Thompson, Lansing and Suellen's 11-year-old daughter and headed back to Phoenix in Thompson's van, where the mood was somber.

Lainer and a male accomplice who has never been identified (Turner and Haynes believed it likely was a Bay Area friend of Lainer's named Robert Coronado) stayed the night at the Rancho Cordova Motel 6, a few miles west of the murder scene.

The day after the murders, the two brazenly drove Riggins' van around on Watt Avenue about 10 miles northwest of the murder scene in broad daylight as a red herring to strengthen the Hunt group's alibi. They wanted to be seen.

Further proof of the Hunts' and Thompson's guilt, Henderson argued, was found in the fact that they all claimed the marriage was in Las Vegas rather than Carson City; that a jailed Gallego filed a discovery motion within days of the murders; that snitch Ray Lopez said he got a full confession from Thompson and actually recorded his "duct tape" comment; and the many similarities between the Riggins-Gonsalves abduction and Hunt's 1985 kidnapping of a young Washington couple.

In short, it was a Hunt-led copycat murder to spring a revered sibling already in jail for a similar crime (a sibling locked up when John and Sabrina were killed, thus shedding doubt on Gallego's involvement in the November 1980 Sowers-Miller murders) who killed to satisfy his lust. If you buy Henderson's theory, it makes the murders of John and Sabrina all the more senseless: they were killed, indirectly, because of Gerald Gallego's perverted libido.

After considerable legal wrangling that would bog down this case time and again, the first preliminary hearing was held in May 1990, a half-year after the arrests. In the months leading up to the hearing, Doug Lainer's role became key to the prosecution. Ever since learning of the $1,000 check that Suellen gave to Lainer on David Hunt's behalf the day before the murders, Fred Turner had been hounding the recovering heroin addict and petty thief. Turner met with Lainer some two dozen times before the preliminary hearing. In October 1989, he told Turner, "I feel guilty for this. I helped Richard Thompson and David Hunt escape and they go out and do this shit."

Neither Turner nor fellow Yolo investigator John Haynes was satisfied with Lainer's original "you'll have to ask them" explanation for the check's purpose. Lainer also did not have an adequate alibi for his whereabouts the day John and Sabrina were killed, according to Turner.

"Lainer tried two or three different alibis," Turner said. "None of them could be proved."

After thinking it over, Lainer told Turner that Hunt owed him the $1,000 for a marijuana business in prison and that he got the money from Suellen, who had money from selling the Bay Area home she owned with her second husband.

"We were dealing a lot of marijuana inside San Quentin," Lainer told me in 2001. "When I got out, (Hunt) knew I didn't have a lot of money, and he wanted to make sure I had enough money to get a place to live. That $1,000 was a combination of drug money and money that he owed me."

Turner and Haynes still weren't buying it. Not only did Lainer's stories not pan out in their estimation, but they also believed they had a witness who put Lainer at the Lucky shopping center on the night of the killings. Rebecca Romani, the Davis woman who saw two suspicious-looking men in a breeze-

Doug Lainer in court after his arrest.

Davis Enterprise

way, who picked Hunt out of a photo lineup in 1987, also, according to investigators, picked out Lainer from a photo lineup as the second man she saw.

Wanting Romani to view Lainer in person, Turner on March 28, 1990, drove Lainer to a police lineup at the Alameda County Jail. On the way, they stopped at a convenience store, where Lainer bought four Colt 45 tall beers and guzzled them in the back of Turner's car as Turner drove. Letting a suspect drink while transporting him to a police lineup was one of many aspects of Turner's overall investigation that was later criticized. "When I picked (Lainer) up for the lineup, he wanted to stop by the store. He didn't tell me he wanted to go in there and buy his daily six-pack," Turner said.

At the lineup, Steven O'Connor, a young lawyer just out of law school, was appointed to represent Lainer. When he asked Haynes to see the police reports, Haynes caviled, saying they amounted to "eight carloads" and it would not be practical. O'Connor then advised Lainer not to participate in the lineup. In yet another bizarre moment in this case, Haynes arrested the attorney on the spot for interfering with an officer. A second attorney allowed the lineup.

Romani remembered a distinct gait by one of the two men she saw looming in the Lucky shopping center breezeway a decade earlier. She asked that the men in the lineup walk. Lainer was designated No. 4 in a six-man lineup. Romani picked No. 3 and No. 4 (Lainer), but said, "It's more three than four."

Three days later, after conferring with Haynes following the lineup, Romani submitted an unusual letter to the Davis police in which she changed her choice to Lainer. "I understand this person is your man," she wrote. "This man is inherently evil...If you look at his eyes, something nasty looks out – he could be out of a Stephen King novel...Please get this guy."

As the preliminary hearing for Suellen and Thompson neared, Haynes and Turner continued to squeeze Lainer, confident that he would give up the others and be a star witness. Haynes said the antsy truck driver came close to confessing on at least two occasions when he was being interrogated, including once when Lainer became so agitated he started peeling off his clothes and throwing them around the room. "I thought for sure he was ready to go," Haynes remembered.

Henderson thought the same thing about Lainer. "I think he was on the brink (of confessing) a couple of times."

Turner and Haynes pushed harder, telling Lainer "it's let's make a deal time" and that he "faced the little green room" in San Quentin's gas chamber if he didn't "play ball."

They even reportedly offered Lainer $50,000, police protection and a new identity to testify against the other three. Like Suellen and Richard Thompson before him, Lainer declined. "They tried to give me deals, they tried to squeeze me," Lainer said. "I told them out of the gate, if I thought these guys did (the murders) I would give them up. But they never believed me. It didn't fit into their theory of the case."

With no deal, Henderson went ahead and subpoenaed Lainer to testify in the preliminary hearing for Suellen and Thompson. As soon as Lainer took the stand, a lawyer for Thompson, aware of the tightrope Lainer walked between witness and suspect, pointed out to Judge Loncke that Lainer should have an attorney. Rod Beede, a Yolo County lawyer who had scant experience representing accused criminals and was on the brink of becoming an adoption attorney, was hastily appointed to represent Lainer at a hearing in Woodland.

"I got to the courthouse, and Doug Lainer is sitting on the front lawn, drunk,"

Beede recalled. "He said, 'They are going to charge me in this case.' "

"They put Doug on the stand, and Henderson told me flat out if Doug didn't 'tell the truth' — which meant if he didn't get on the stand and turn Richard Thompson and David Hunt — he was going to charge him with murder."

And that's what happened. After Lainer refused to testify on the grounds that he might incriminate himself (Lainer said he had nothing to hide and merely followed Beede's on-the-fly advice) Turner and Haynes arrested Lainer on May 29, 1990, in the hallway of the Yolo County Courthouse in Woodland. The detectives reportedly slapped handcuffs on an infuriated Lainer as he flopped around on the floor.

There were now four suspects charged with first-degree murder with special circumstances. Because Henderson sought the death penalty, each defendant was entitled by California law to two court-appointed attorneys and an investigator. The People had one attorney, the defense eight. Henderson had his work cut out for him.

Lainer's prelim was combined with David Hunt's in the fall of 1990. While Romani's identification of Lainer seemed shaky at best, Henderson had a new witness in the wings. The witness, Katherine Bernard,* was sure she saw Lainer driving Riggins' van the day after the killings west of the murder site and not far from the Arden Fair shopping center where Miller and Sowers were abducted. She would be among a handful of key witnesses who testified at the two prelims.

Dozens of witnesses were called to support Henderson's theory, including Gallego's ex-wife Charlene, testifying between sobs that Gallego was very interested in the Davis killings and "very adamant" about filing a discovery motion within days of the murders.

While many witnesses helped lay the foundation of Henderson's theory, the case largely boiled down to the testimony of four people: Valerie Thompson, William Lansing, Ray Lopez, and Bernard.

A father of five, Lansing was the Phoenix neighbor of Hunt and the Thompsons in December 1980, the outlaw wannabe who tagged along with the two convicts. Lansing gave damaging if vague testimony. He recounted the odd blood ritual that took place before the trip to Carson City, saw Hunt and Thompson carrying knives in Carson City, remembered Hunt putting on a wig and disguise as they reached Carson City, and could not vouch for the Hunts' and Richard Thompson's whereabouts the night of Dec. 20. Lansing testified he was dropped off at the Nugget casino about 6 or 7 p.m., but did

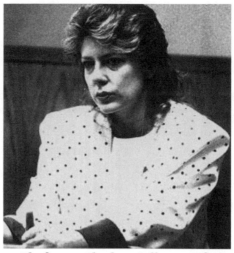

The former Charlene Gallego testifying.

Davis Enterprise

not recall how he got there or who took him. He did not know what happened to Thompson, whom he called "Jimbo," or the Hunts (he called David Hunt "Billy") after going to the casino.

Q: "When did you next see Jimbo, Billy or Sue?"

A: "That next morning."

Q: "About what time?"

A: "About 8."

Q: "Before you went to the casino, before you separated from Jimbo, Billy and Sue, did any of them say what they were going to do that night?"

A: "Not that I recall."

Q: "Mr. Lansing, do you recall Billy telling you, 'We have family business to take care of'"?

A: "Yes, I do."

Q: "What else do you recall being said in the context of 'We have family business to take care of'?"

A: "I assumed because they just got married. That is what I thought they meant."

Henderson then asked Lansing what happened the next morning after he met up with Thompson and the Hunts. Lansing testified that the mood darkened after the group packed up Thompson's van and headed to Phoenix.

"On the way up, people were laid-back. Everybody was joking. On the way back, everybody was uptight about something."

Lansing's credibility and ability to remember were challenged by the defense. He admitted alcohol clouded his recollection of events after being dropped off at the casino.

Q: "You got drunk that night, didn't you?"

A: "More than likely, yes."

Q: "You don't remember how you got back from the casino to the motel?"

A: "No, I don't."

Q: "And you don't know which room you woke up at in the motel?"

A: "No, I don't."

Q: "Is that because you were drunk?"

A: "Probably."

Lansing was followed on the stand at the first prelim by informant Ray Lopez. Despite being in a room with suspects who likely wanted to wring his neck, Lopez had a swagger in his step and seemed confident on the stand. Lopez explained to the court how he thought Hunt might be behind the killings when media first reported them.

"It was just so close," Lopez reasoned. "His (Hunt's) brother, Gallego, killed these two kids, and a short time later these two other kids get killed."

Lopez recounted his unrecorded conversation with Thompson that elicited the alleged confession in the bar.

Q: "Did Mr. Thompson tell you how the two victims were killed?"

A: "Yeah. He said that Mr. Hunt killed the male. That he killed the female. That John Riggins evidently put up some sort of struggle and David calmed him down real quick."

Q: "Did Mr. Thompson indicate that either of the victims had said anything prior to being killed?"

A: "He indicated that Sabrina Gonsalves pleaded with him to not kill her. And he stated they all do that before they die."

Q: "Did you ask why Sabrina Gonsalves had not been raped?"

A: "Because Mr. Hunt's wife was following him there; that was the only reason she wasn't raped. She had followed them in her car, and that Sue Hunt didn't see the bodies because 'she was skittish.'"

The defense chipped away at Lopez's character on cross-examination. Lopez, who has a long rapsheet, admitted he had been arrested for a domestic dispute with his girlfriend, that he was being paid for some of his information for the Riggins-Gonsalves case, and that he was interested in the considerable reward money.

More damning testimony came from Valerie Thompson, who got immunity from prosecution in exchange for recounting her version of events the weekend of Dec. 20, 1980. A frumpy, frizzy-haired woman, Valerie detailed her role in the dramatic San Quentin escape. Henderson then asked about the blood ritual in the Phoenix apartments the night before the group departed Arizona for Carson City.

"Richard Thompson was drunk and acting strange and out of control," she said. "David Hunt was trying to get some control over Richard Thompson, and in the process of the blood brother ritual...David Hunt grabbed my wrist and cut it. He grabbed Richard Thompson's wrist and cut it. And he cut himself, at which point the blood was mingled, and that was it."

Q: "Would you describe what Richard Thompson was doing as unusual?"

A: "Yeah. He threw himself into the landlord's Christmas tree. He jumped into the console stereo. He babbled incoherently. When I was walking him from the landlord's house, he was walking all over the place and talking disjointedly. It didn't make sense...Later, he started talking in colors and numbers in the apartment."

Up until his ex-wife's testimony, Richard Thompson sat calmly with a crooked grin on his weathered face. Court observers described him as "mousy" and a "hermit." But as Valerie testified, his face tightened with anger and he methodically beat a clenched fist against a chair leg. Henderson pressed

**Richard Thompson in court following his
arrest for the murders.**

Davis Enterprise

for more details on the blood ritual. Valerie said it seemed to be some sort of bonding between Hunt and Thompson and that Thompson did not want her privy to it.

"He wanted me gone. He wanted to leave me behind," she said. Valerie added that Hunt included her in the ritual and wanted her to go on to Carson City because she was Thompson's wife, and that she and Hunt stayed up washing blood off the bedding after Thompson passed out drunk.

Like Lansing, Valerie was asked about the whereabouts of Hunt, Suellen and Thompson following the wedding. And like Lansing, she could not provide them an alibi.

Q: "Do you recall the three returning that evening?"

A: "No, I don't remember their return."

Q: "Do you recall telling Detective Turner that after you got to Carson City you were fairly much left out of everything?"

A: "Yes."

Q: "And that Sue, David and Richard did everything together?"

A: "Pretty much."

Q: "Do you remember telling Detective Turner that on this trip to Carson City and especially after the marriage, both Richard Thompson and David Hunt had closed you off like a curtain that dropped between you?"

A: "Very likely, yes."

Q: "They were not conversing with you and you really did not know what was going on?"

A: "That is true."

Also like Lansing, Valerie testified about a different mood in the van on the way back to Phoenix, noting that Hunt "appeared to be upset" and arguing with Suellen.

The former girlfriend of Thompson's, Diana Sherman, gave testimony that could have devastated the defense. Sherman accompanied Thompson to two police interviews in 1987, during which the fingerprints found in Riggins' van were mentioned. Sherman testified that following the interviews, she asked Thompson, "Did you ever take your gloves off?" – and Thompson replied, "No." She further told the court that she asked Thompson, "You did it, didn't you?" – and Thompson didn't respond.

It was perhaps the most damning testimony in the hearing. But Sherman, characterized by the defense as vindictive over a romantic spat with Thompson, later recanted it.

At closing arguments of the preliminary hearing for Suellen and Thompson, Henderson focused on the inconsistencies in their alibis the weekend of the murders:

"It's very important that Mrs. Hunt went into the effort of lying about what she did after the wedding," Henderson told the court. "She did not go back to Phoenix. She did not spend the night in Phoenix. Her alibi is blown and her effort to provide false evidence of her location is irrefutable proof of her responsibility as a co-conspirator in these killings.

"Bill Lansing and Valerie Thompson showed absolutely no confusion that the trip was planned for Carson City from the outset, and that that was the only location, the only destination. They had no information about Las Vegas being an integral part of the trip. And yet, of the three people who proof shows were responsible, all three of them insist that they were in Las Vegas, which provides them with an alibi. There is no rational conclusion that could be derived from this intensity by the three co-conspirators that they were in Las Vegas, other than they constructed an alibi as a way to protect themselves from responsibility for what they did on the evening of Dec. 20."

The defense countered that there were no sightings of either Suellen or Thompson in California the weekend in question. Dennis Tanabe, appointed to defend Suellen, said his client married David Hunt so she would not have to testify in the San Quentin escape, not, as Turner alleged, to get spousal immunity for the murders. He also suggested that the $1,000 check to Lainer was for his role as messenger in the escape and had no part in the murders.

"There isn't any law against someone being in love with someone who commits crimes," Tanabe said. "And my client, unfortunately, is in the position where she is associated with someone (Hunt) against whom there is evidence."

Judge Loncke characterized the killings as "murders most foul."

While he commended the "persistence of the investigating officers," the judge also noted that "the prosecution of this case in the beyond-the-reasonable-doubt standard will present immense difficulties for the prosecution." He nevertheless bound Thompson and Suellen over for trial and ordered them back to jail without bail.

Hunt and Lainer's preliminary hearing, held in September and October 1990, was largely a rerun of Suellen and Thompson's. Most of the same witnesses testified again, only this time there were more theatrics and more problems with the prosecution's witnesses.

Lainer, wound so tightly that his attorneys used to take him out to shoot baskets at the county jail basketball court just to calm him down enough to be able to talk to him, had a hard time containing his anger in the courtroom. On one occasion, he hung over the wood partition in front of the spectator section, and barked at Sabrina's mother, Kim. "Who are the family members?" he said, facing the gallery.

"I am," replied Kim Gonsalves.

"They've got the wrong guy!"

At a court hearing in October, Lainer, in chains and accompanied by two security guards, lunged at Henderson and warned him he would kill him once he got out of prison.

"I wanted to jump up and whip the man," Lainer admitted to me.

Hunt, meanwhile, kept his cool, rarely showing emotion, and his cocky machismo seemed to impress women. Suellen, who eyed him lovingly the few times the two appeared in court together, wasn't the only one drawn to the career outlaw: an attractive young paralegal on the defense side openly flirted with him in court. The Davis Enterprise even ran a picture of the pretty brunette whispering in a grinning Hunt's ear. "We showed that picture to Suellen in jail to get her jealous," Turner said in 2000. Investigators also sent female informants into jail posing as prisoners to elicit a confession from Suellen. Nothing came of it.

Much of Hunt and Lainer's preliminary hearing focused on the testimony and credibility of Katherine Bernard. In the spring of 1990, Bernard informed authorities that she saw the Riggins van driving on Sacramento's Watt Avenue on the day after the murders as she drove her Chevy Caprice to her workplace to deliver Christmas baskets to co-workers. Lonely and depressed about being by herself at the holidays, she said she routinely kept an eye out for unique license plates to entertain herself. On the day after the killings, she distinctly remembered the 3S MUM license plate because she thought it stood for see/hear/speak no evil. She also said she saw a blue car trailing the van, which is consistent with other witness accounts.

Well-mannered, well-dressed and very nervous, Bernard gave testimony that if true, was another black mark in the Sacramento County Sheriff's Department's investigation of the case. She told the court that she reported the van sighting back in March 1981, but the Sheriff's Department showed "absolutely no interest."

"I told my ex-husband in a letter, 'I very probably am the only one who can truly identify the driver of that van, and they are not going to let me do it,' " she testified.

But Bernard kept notes of the sighting, held onto them for years. And when she was contacted by Turner, Bernard picked Lainer out of a photo lineup as the van's driver. Bernard testified that the van's driver seemed to go out of his way to be seen when she pulled up alongside the van at the intersection of Watt Avenue and Arden Way the day after the killings.

Q: "Were you able to see the driver of the van as it made its U-turn?"

A: "Yes."

Q: "Did the driver do anything unusual?"

A: "Yes...I followed the driver with my eyes all the way around the turn. And I guess I was staring, but I was getting a good look at him. All of a sudden he made a face at me, like, 'Take a good look.'...It was the meanest face I ever saw."

Q: "Is the person that you saw driving the van in court today?"

A: "Yes, he is.

Q: "Would you point him out?'

Bernard pointed to Lainer: "He is seated over there in blue at the end of that table."

Lainer's defense team worked hard to discredit the identification, maintaining the van was never moved once it was abandoned on Folsom Boulevard across from Aerojet. An Aerojet security guard testified that on the Sunday that Bernard claimed to have seen the van being driven around, he came to work just before 7 a.m. and noticed the van parked under a tree. When he left work at 3:15 p.m., the guard said the van appeared to be in the same exact spot. If both the guard and Bernard are to be believed, Lainer got in the van after 7 a.m. Sunday morning, drove it around during the noon hour, then returned it to the same spot before the guard left work at 3:15 p.m. There was some speculation on Henderson's part that Lainer may have even spent the night of Dec. 20 sleeping in the van.

Bernard also testified that the van's driver was clean-cut in appearance: friends of Lainer's testified that he had a mustache and long hair during the period in question. A traffic engineer was even brought in to testify at length that the Watt Avenue traffic lights were not timed the way Bernard described them when she allegedly idled next to the van on Dec. 21, 1980.

Judge Loncke nevertheless allowed Bernard's identification of Lainer, calling it "a startlingly conclusive identification." It was a victory for the prosecution, one of the few rulings that went Henderson's way in the second hearing.

While there never were any witness identifications of Suellen or Thompson in Davis or Sacramento, Henderson maintained he had solid identifications of Hunt, including one by Kelly James, the motorist who saw a suspicious man walking on Folsom Boulevard near Rudy's Hideaway about 10 the night of the slayings. Looking at Hunt in the courtroom, James testified that he "resembled" the man she saw that night.

But in a significant setback, Judge Loncke threw out the testimony of two key witnesses, Rebecca Romani and Joyce Hullender.

Hullender, the motorist who peeked into the Riggins van the night of the murders after it blocked her route on Folsom Boulevard, gave credible testimony on the van's appearance and what she saw inside of it: strewn papers, gloves and a baseball cap. But her identification of a man she may or may not have seen that night began to unravel on the witness stand. Hullender initially reported in 1980 she heard footsteps at the rear of the van but didn't see anybody. She later changed her mind, saying she actually saw a face of a man at the rear of the van. In 1987, she picked Hunt out of a photo lineup.

Trembling as she testified, she looked at Hunt and identified him as the man she saw lurking in the fog near the van. She also noted that the man she claimed to have seen by the van had eyes that "looked empty" — a description of Hunt's eyes expressed by others.

But Judge Loncke grew wary of Hullender. Not only was there the discrepancy between what she first reported and what she later told Turner, but it was learned that she participated in a police lineup without her glasses, couldn't really see a thing, but nevertheless picked a man (not Hunt) "because I was afraid not to put down something." Citing inconsistencies in Hullender's story and identifications, Judge Loncke dismissed her testimony and therefore, her ID of Hunt.

He did the same thing with Romani's alleged identification of Lainer. The judge noted Romani's bizarre letter to the police in which she changed her identification to Lainer after choosing another man over Lainer in the live lineup. He also pointed out inconsistencies between her 1980 report to police and her testimony 10 years later, namely that her original report described the men she saw as being quite a bit younger than Hunt and Lainer were in 1980.

Romani was a feisty witness. She didn't back down from tough questions by the defense and even counterpunched to the delight of observers who found the defense attorneys overly aggressive. Defense attorneys, on the other hand, had no shortage of disparaging remarks for Romani's testimony. Hunt attorney Barry Newman, for one, called it "the most ludicrous thing I ever saw." Judge Loncke seemed to agree at least somewhat, deeming Romani's testimony unreliable, saying it reflected "an imagination that ran rampant."

The prosecution suffered yet another blow when Loncke also tossed testimony on Hunt's 1985 kidnapping of the Washington couple, despite Henderson claiming there were 25 points of similarity between the two cases and considerable testimony from witnesses, including the Washington kidnap victims themselves. Steven Skuza testified that he was kidnapped at gunpoint, taped with silver duct tape, beaten, and cut with knives. His girlfriend, Kirsten Baugher, testified that Hunt bound her with tape and raped her.

However, Russell Vorpagel, an expert in police procedure, testified that "In my comparison of the two cases the similarities were so general and they were not that important to me...I came to the conclusion that the two crimes could not be committed by the same person."

It wasn't just witnesses. Fred Turner underwent a grueling cross-examination about his aggressive investigation techniques. The Davis detective was grilled about the inaccuracies in his affidavits, particularly the misstatement implying that Lopez recorded a full confession by Thompson, when in fact the informant simply claimed to have heard a confession. Turner's relative lack of homicide experience — just a handful of cases throughout his career — was exposed, and he admitted to a lack of formal training in such areas as showing witnesses photo lineups, which he relied on heavily.

Turner kept his cool on the witness stand despite hours of tough questions, including some by Hunt lawyer Hayes Gable III that shed doubt on the Lucky shopping center as the abduction site.

Q: "Do you have any witnesses whatsoever that saw them being abducted from the Lucky supermarket?"

A: "No."

Q: "So you don't really have any evidence that they were abducted from the parking lot, do you?"

A: "No."

Q: "Do you have any facts at your disposal?"

A: "I have no witnesses. I have no physical evidence."

Despite the setbacks, Henderson forged on. In a dramatic closing argument, he recounted his theory, making a point about probabilities in the two sets of murders that to this day makes them a very strange coincidence, at least.

"How many times in the history of Northern California have kids from the age of 18 to 23, male/female sweethearts, Caucasian, been kidnapped from a shopping center and ended up dead east of Sacramento?" the DA said. "What likelihood does it have? Is it pure coincidence that these abductions and killings took place between the span of Nov. 2, 1980, and Dec. 20, some 48 days later, and were done by totally independent factors?

"That exceeds the possibility of purely happenstance. It suggests that there is a common factor, a common force that has ruled in these deaths."

In its closing arguments, the defense continued to hammer at the witnesses' credibility. Lainer attorney Beede maintained his client was being punished simply for not having any information. He suggested that Valerie Thompson and outlaw-wannabe-tagalong Bill Lansing had more culpability than Lainer because they were with the Carson City wedding party. Lainer, Beede argued, "had nothing they could use, so they cram him into the theory. And the way they cram him into the theory is to bring him before the court and hope that somewhere down the line it will just get too intense. He will break and give them what they want to hear."

Hunt attorney Gable labeled Henderson's theory a "fairy tale" and said the logistics involved in the alleged three-state murder plan were farfetched. "This whole scenario, it is kind of like a commando raid, the way the prosecution has put it together. You have people coming from all different directions, meetings, carrying on, planned action with split-second precision, because they have to be back, they have to drive a certain distance.

"They all knew to meet in Davis, California, at a nondescript shopping center that isn't even close in size and proximity to the metropolitan Sacramento area, and the Arden Fair shopping center. The only thing similar is that it was a male and female. Nobody knows if (the abduction) took place at the shopping center. It could just have easily taken place at Ms. Gonsalves' (condo). It is on the same route."

Gable mocked the notion that the van was driven around by Lainer after the killings.

The Hunt group "had supposedly kidnapped these people, and for all they knew, the entire police force was looking for them...it doesn't make any sense at all, none at all — why do they need to have that van removed, driven around and put right back in that spot?"

Judge Loncke, a distinguished jurist who was named Judge of the Year by the Sacramento County Bar Association in 1991, had a lot to mull over. He had on several occasions with preliminary hearings found insufficient evidence to hold the accused over for trial. But ultimately, he seemed to agree with what a lot of court observers believed: The Hunt party had the motive and they had the opportunity to kill John and Sabrina – and they didn't have a strong alibi for their whereabouts the night of Dec. 20, 1980.

"Through diligent police work, a chilling, believable story evolves that is no fairy tale," Loncke said with a veiled dig at Gable's "fairy tale" comment. "John Riggins and Sabrina Gonsalves were selected as targets of opportunity, and for this most heinous purpose were cruelly murdered. The blood ritual in Phoenix, the selection of Carson City as the marriage location, and the leaving behind of William Lansing 'in order to take care of family business' are evidence of this conspiracy."

The case against Hunt, the judge noted, was "overwhelming."

Lainer's connection to the murders, he cautioned, was "murkier." But he suspected some involvement.

"When considered with the rest of the evidence regarding Mr. Lainer's involvement with the escape from San Quentin, his contacts with Sue Hunt during the period immediately before and after the Dec. 20 abduction, it gives rise to strong suspicion that he was a person viewed driving the 3S MUM van by Mrs. Bernard," Loncke said.

The judge then ordered both Hunt and Lainer to stand trial for the murders.

"At best," he said, "justice will ultimately be served with the appropriate punishment of those responsible for the murders of Sabrina Gonsalves and John Riggins."

22
Circus

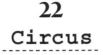

The wheels of justice in the Riggins-Gonsalves case seemed finally to be inching forward when all four members of the Hunt party were bound over for trial in 1990. Those wheels nearly fell off, however, with a series of tragicomic delays and legal maneuvers that bogged down the case so many times it teetered on collapsing under its own weight.

By seeking the death penalty against four suspects who were entitled to two attorneys each, Yolo County District Attorney David Henderson created an eight-headed defense juggernaut that came at him from four directions, jabbing him with one motion after another. "I don't think they wanted to go to trial," said Henderson, who did a fair amount of legal maneuvering himself. "They had four or five different motions that said the police and DA were bad people and violated their due process."

In early 1991, David and Suellen Hunt and Richard Thompson moved to have the charges dismissed, contending that their rights to a speedy trial were denied because too much time had elapsed between the killings and the arrests. They said key witnesses had died or couldn't recount pertinent facts, that important documents were lost.

Knowing that David Hunt had been fingered as a possible suspect just days after the murders, defense attorneys put Sacramento County Sheriff's Lt. Ray Biondi on the witness stand in Yolo County Superior Court and asked the lanky, highly regarded detective a question that is still asked to this day:

Why didn't you really go after this guy when you first heard about him?

"He was just another name on a long list of suspects we were working on," Biondi calmly told the court. "We were looking for harder information that linked (the Hunt group) to the crime. We didn't have that."

Biondi knew early on of the Gallego copycat theory, but testified that he "did not evaluate it as being viable."

"In fact, it was kind of dismissed as being suspect information, so it was not actively worked on, with the exception of an interview of David (by Sacramento Detective Stan Reed) when (Hunt) was in our jail."

The motion to drop the charges was denied, though it did put another boulder in Henderson's path, as did a motion by Suellen and David Hunt that the Yolo DA violated their civil rights by illegally screening their mail. While Yolo jail guards routinely screened inmates' mail, the Hunts' was plucked from the usual routing and forwarded to Henderson and his lead investigators on the case, Fred Turner and John Haynes. In defending the screening, Henderson cited David Hunt's history of prison escapes and claimed the Hunts communicated in hidden codes. "There are ongoing investigations into what we believe to be current escape conspiracies," Henderson said.

An expert who monitored mail at Folsom Prison testified that the Hunts did indeed communicate surreptitiously via codes, pictures and even a Calvin and Hobbes comic. He explained that they communicated via "talk-around" – a combination of words and symbols to convey hidden messages.

Unconvinced, Yolo County Judge James Roach ordered the DA to cease the unprecedented censorship, ruling that the jail's normal screening procedures sufficed. Suellen said the notes were innocent love letters. "David was very into American Indians. And he would write suns and mountains and little love things, and (the prosecution) tried to decide that this was a code."

The legal wrangling and delays, including medical care for the suspects, continued. David Hunt had a hernia operation – under heavy guard as it was feared he would try to escape – that slowed his case. Defense attorneys lost a bid to disqualify Judge Roach from hearing Thompson's case. Douglas Lainer's attorneys filed several motions: one sought resumption of methadone treatments that he said were cut off to expedite a confession, one asked for dismissal of murder charges because of alleged police misconduct by Turner and Haynes, one sought to prevent Lainer's participation in a pretrial police lineup, and another asked that he be tried separately from David Hunt out of concern of being tainted by the "damning" evidence against Hunt.

Suellen, a first-time prisoner who complained about everything from the county jail's food to her ill-fitting inmate clothes, in 1990 filed a lawsuit claiming false arrest. Alarmed by all the media attention, David Hunt's legal team filed a motion contending that the extraordinary publicity in the case – there were hundreds of newspaper articles alone – prevented the defendants from getting a fair trial.

Media experts testified that the media coverage was prejudicial, that David Hunt's name had been strongly linked to sex slayer Gerald Gallego, and that

A handcuffed Suellen being led into court.
Davis Enterprise

John and Sabrina had essentially been elevated to saint status in Davis. A poll of Yolo County residents showed that 34 percent of those familiar with the case believed David Hunt was guilty or likely guilty.

"I sat in that courtroom and watched the Gonsalves family just staring at me with such hatred," Suellen recalled.

And, testified media analyst Craig Haney, "This is the strangest case I've ever seen in terms of the number of articles and the saturation of the community." Haney also noted that Henderson had politicized the case by mentioning it in his 1990 re-election campaign, by wondering if his opponent would have the experience to prosecute the case.

In late 1991, Judge Roach ruled that David Hunt and Thompson, set to be tried first, could not receive a fair trial in Yolo County. The trial was moved to Santa Rosa in Sonoma County. Befitting a case where nothing came easy, Sonoma County did not want what promised to be a long — possibly one of the longest in California history — and messy trial in its courthouse. "Sonoma County was not happy about us showing up there," Henderson said.

And Henderson was not happy with the judge assigned to the case in

Sonoma. Henderson accused Judge John Keane, a retired Sierra County jurist, of sleeping during the pretrial hearings and interrupting them with coughing fits.

Henderson moved to disqualify the 72-year-old Keane, who claimed to be fine despite some obvious infirmities. "I was really concerned (Keane) wasn't going to make it," Henderson recalled. "A couple of times he coughed so much he had to go out of sight behind the bench. And then he'd come back up. He had also learned this technique where he could actually sit with his chin in his hand with his eyes closed."

Hunt and Thompson wanted separate trials. A compromise of sorts was reached when it was ruled that the trials could be consolidated, but with two juries. In what promised to be an unwieldy game of legal musical chairs, the juries would hear some of the testimony together, some of it separately.

"Dual juries in this case will be a two-ring circus," Hunt attorney Hayes Gable complained to the press. It was an apt analogy for a case that had more legal motions than you could swing a gavel at.

Two juries for one case. Alleged codes in mail exchanges. Publicity bumping the case to a county that wanted nothing to do with it. A sleeping judge. More than 10,000 pages of discovery and 200-plus audio tapes. Mounting costs to the taxpayers.

By 1992, the circus had come to Santa Rosa in the form of a bloated Riggins-Gonsalves trial, a showcase of the weird. And it was about to get even weirder.

23
Blanket
----

*"I want a trial. I have been in jail three years and three months with
everyone in the world thinking I'm the bogeyman."*

— David Hunt

It looks so innocent and cheerful, a stark contrast to the evil secret it contained the only time it was used. Solid light blue on one side, a festive red
and dark blue paisley swirl on the other. It is 64 inches long by 56 inches
wide, cotton, with polyester fill and fasteners. It was supposedly purchased
at Macy's in Sacramento, back when Davisites routinely did their Christmas
shopping in Sacramento.

Feminine, practical and, thanks to the paisley, very 1970s, it was the big
gift for Andrea Gonsalves's 22nd birthday, something sensible she could get
cozy in during the energy crisis while grading papers. It was *so* Sabrina.

The blue "bundle-up blanket" as it became known in police vernacular,
was wrapped inside of three boxes as a gag and loaded in the back of the
Riggins van on Dec. 20, 1980. John and Sabrina placed it in the van in what
may have been the last carefree moment of their lives.

When police found the van two days later, the blanket had been plucked
out of its clear plastic wrapping and left wadded up between the driver's
captain's chair and the front passenger's bench seat.

The blanket was hastily checked into the Sacramento County District
Attorney's evidence room along with other things strewn about the vehicle,
including the ice cream containers; Andrea's birthday card; a Soda Springs
trail map; a Mobil Oil Co. gas receipt; a gas cap; some cough drops; a fishing
weight; a handkerchief; a rubber whistle thought to belong to Sabrina; and a
book of matches from the Sidney Hotel in Sidney, British Columbia.

The day after the van and bodies were found, investigators forwarded
the blanket and handkerchief to the Sacramento County Crime Lab for an

**The blanket as it was discovered in the van.
(The ice cream is in the bag on the floor.)**

examination of bodily fluids. While DNA profiling would not be introduced in criminal cases until 1986, technology existed since the 1940s to detect semen via an enzyme unique to it and by typing it like blood – A, B or O.

When Fred Turner started investigating the case in 1987, he asked Sacramento County Homicide Detective Stan Reed about the blanket. Reed told Turner the same thing he told me when I first asked him about the blanket in 2001: That he oversaw crime lab analyst Ken Mack's inspection of it – and nothing unusual was detected. "I was standing right there looking at it," Reed said.

In June 1989, Turner submitted the blanket to the California Department of Justice crime lab and asked for a "trace evidence" inspection. "I expected them to search for traces of anything – blood, hair, fiber, semen," Turner recalled. "Nothing was found."

He probably should have asked the lab for a semantics lesson as well. Unknown to Turner, the lab's definition of "trace evidence" did not include an inspection for bodily fluids. For that, one must ask for a serological examination. While Turner did not make such a specific request after the Hunt group was arrested, Sacramento investigators did ask for a serological inspection on the blanket when it was originally checked into the evidence room in 1980. This request was apparently ignored or forgotten.

With nothing notable found on the blanket, Turner focused on the other evidence. The Rigginses had no idea how a matchbook from British Columbia got into their van. In his investigation of Suellen, Turner learned that in the early 1970s she had been in British Columbia tending to her then father-in-law, who had a stroke. Perhaps, Turner surmised, the matches had come from Suellen, maybe put in the van as a red herring to further throw off the investigation. Yolo investigator John Haynes, on the other hand, thought maybe Hunt and Thompson picked up the matches during their Pacific Northwest crime spree in November 1980.

After Sacramento County declined to prosecute the Hunt group, Turner transferred the evidence from Sacramento to the Davis Police Department's evidence room. It sat there in a cardboard box as the prosecution and defense jostled in preparation for what promised to be a long, dramatic trial in Sonoma County, set to start sometime in 1992.

Yolo DA David Henderson built his case on a compelling sequence of circumstantial evidence, not physical evidence. There was no murder weapon, no matching fingerprints. As far as he knew from his information from both Turner and Sacramento County, there was nothing of particular import on the items found in the van, nothing unusual on the blue blanket or the handkerchief that was left behind.

Besides, the Sacramento County pathologist who did Sabrina's autopsy testified at the prelim that there was no sign of sexual assault. "I'd assumed what the Sacramento authorities initially reported was correct," Henderson said.

Turner figured the blanket was taken out of its wrapper and used to cover the victims in transit from Davis to Sacramento. After all, there was pretrial testimony from more than one witness that something was covering one of the van's windows — including while the van was seen swerving on the Yolo Causeway.

With their clients facing the death penalty, defense attorneys wanted a fresh look at the evidence. They asked that the blanket, handkerchief, the victims' clothes and other items be examined using technologies that, by 1992, were exponentially more advanced than they were in 1980. There was now DNA testing.

In June 1992, Henderson had Davis police resubmit the items to the DOJ lab with a specific request for a serological examination — which includes bodily fluids. The evidence was turned over to Faye Springer, a highly regarded forensics expert known for her work on the "I-5 Killer" case of the mid-1980s (in which Roger Kibbe was identified as the prime suspect in a series of abductions and sex stranglings near Sacramento), and several other high-profile murders.

Springer flipped through the police reports. She thought it odd that the new blanket was found out of its package in the van. "It was pretty peculiar. I mean, if you were just killing somebody or robbing them, why would you open this blanket? So either (the killers) were opening it to steal it and decided they didn't want it, or used it for some part of the crime."

Using nothing more than her eyes, Springer inspected the comforter. What she found was astounding: Four semen stains on the solid light-blue side. Not only that, but semen stains that Springer said were "pretty obvious."

The yellowish stains seemed old and were spaced several inches apart: It appeared an ejaculation spread to different points on the blanket after it was folded.

Next, Springer looked at John and Sabrina's clothes. Surprisingly, this apparently was the first time the clothes had been closely inspected in the 11-plus years since they were removed from the bodies. In fact, the victims' families got letters in August 1981 informing them that if they did not pick up the clothes within eight days, the clothes (which ended up being kept in an evidence room) would be destroyed. "I don't think the clothing had been looked at prior to me getting it," Springer said.

Springer pored over the clothes. Again, another startling discovery: Sabrina's panties had a number of stains that tested positive for acid phosphatase, a component of semen. But unlike the blanket stains, no intact spermatozoa or seminal proteins were detected at this time. Springer also found a shoe-print on the panties, possibly from a boot.

The stains and shoeprint were detected on the inside of panties that were found inside-out on Sabrina's body, i.e. they were on the outside of the garment when she was found. One possible explanation of the boot print is that Sabrina was kicked into the ravine (this may also explain her vaginal bruise).

Springer also planned to look at the "rape kits" for the victims — envelopes containing rectal, vaginal and oral swabs from Sabrina and rectal and oral swabs from John. She carefully opened the envelopes. Empty. All that fell out was a small amount of cotton in Sabrina's vaginal swab envelope. It was examined for the sperm. None was found.

She also noted a hair found on John's sweater that matched Hunt's in appearance.

Suddenly, after more than 11 years, there was a seismic shift in the case.

Sperm on the blue comforter. What appeared to be sperm on Sabrina's

4400 V Street • Sacramento, California 95817

GEORGE L. NIELSEN • Coroner • Public Administrator • Public Guardian • Public Conservator

COUNTY OF SACRAMENTO

CORONER
PUBLIC ADMINISTRATOR
PUBLIC GUARDIAN
PUBLIC CONSERVATOR

8-6-51

Dr. Richard Riggins
1112 Bucknell
Davis, Ca 95841

Re: John Riggins   , Deceased

Dear Dr. Riggins

We are holding in this office property of the above named
decedent who passed away on _12-22-80_ . The
property consists of the following:

☐ Jewelry

☐ Miscellaneous property

☐ Money

☒ Clothing (Box # _377_)

If this property is not claimed by you or someone authorized
in writing by you by _8-14-81_ , the property will be
disposed of by this office.

Sincerely,

GEORGE L. NIELSEN, Coroner

By: _Sharon Brazelton_
Deputy

Coroner 440-5000 • Public Administrator 440-5422 • Public Guardian 440-5425 • Public Conservator 440-5425 • Toxicology Laboratory 440-5433

Clothes note sent to the Riggineses by Sacramento County in 1981.
The Gonsalveses got a similar note requesting that their daughter's
clothes be retrieved – or they would be destroyed.

panties. Missing rape kits. How could this be?

There was no explanation for the empty rape kits. They remain a mystery, though Springer speculated the samples may have been used up during previous testing. If so, nobody bothered to document it. The blanket? It was never inspected in 1981 as originally thought, though investigators had made out a note requesting a check for serological fluids. Evidence rooms tend to get overwhelmed by the enormous amount of property seized in crimes, and much of it isn't always very closely tracked once it's brought in.

"We learned the hard way that the detective should go to the crime lab with the criminalist and inspect the submitted items and discuss what examinations are possible," Ray Biondi noted. "For years we tried to get the crime lab independent or under the Sheriff's Department. The Sacramento County crime lab is part of the DA's office, and consequently the priority is evidence in solved cases going to court."

When the blanket was slated for inspection, the case was going nowhere. Although Stan Reed told Turner — and later, me — that he and criminalist Ken Mack visually inspected the blanket in 1981, Reed later acknowledged that isn't quite right.

At my request in 2001, Reed went back and found the report he wrote concerning the blanket on March 19, 1981. The report said Mack had the blanket on an exam table. Reed noticed the blanket had vegetation consistent with the ravine where the bodies were found. But that's as far as he went. The blanket was folded and Reed did not want to handle it because Mack told him he was going to inspect it at a later time.

"I'm assuming Mack would have collected samples off of (the blanket) and probably looked at it in ultraviolet light in search of semen or whatever," Reed said. "But evidently he did not do that."

Either way, the discovery of semen on the blanket and perhaps in Sabrina's panties, while startling, was welcome news for the prosecution. This new information, perhaps combined with Sabrina's vaginal bruise, strongly suggested Sabrina was sexually assaulted. And if Sabrina was assaulted, the murders were even more similar to sex slayer Gerald Gallego's than originally thought. Henderson's copycat theory had new legs.

Additionally, there was now physical evidence that could strongly link the suspects to the crime. With a death penalty trial nearing in Santa Rosa, the noose appeared to be tightening on the Hunt party.

Lainer attorney Rod Beede, who, despite being part of the defense, had serious doubts about Hunt and Thompson's innocence at this time ("I spent years figuring they did it," he said), recalled Fred Turner's excitement about the discovery. "He was absolutely sure, excited and thrilled that the stain had been found. This was it, he assured me, one of (the suspects' DNA) would be on it and that was all there was to (the Hunt party's guilt), it was a done deal. Time for the 'little green room' – cyanide all around."

DNA blood samples from the suspects were collected: When technicians struggled to find a vein in David Hunt's arm, Hunt angrily grabbed the syringe and plunged it into the back of his hand, blood spurting. "Here's your sample," he growled.

Distrustful of each other, the defense and prosecution divided the blanket samples and sent them to separate laboratories. Because the semen was degraded, an exact DNA identification – the type that produces one-in-a-billion "cold hits" – was not possible at that time.

Rather, the DNA that could be extracted used the polymerase chain reaction (PCR) typing method. This method doesn't so much identify as exclude: The DNA taken from the blanket could be found in as much as 1.9 percent of the Caucasian population – the race for the three male suspects and John Riggins.

The defense results came back first, in November 1992. There were four samples from the blanket that were submitted to the Serological Research Institute in San Francisco along with blood DNA samples from the victims and the suspects. Gary C. Harmor, a respected forensic serologist who did the tests, could only detect microscopic DNA on two of the samples.

But it was enough.

"John Riggins, Douglas Lainer, Richard Thompson and David Hunt *could not* be the donors of the stains on the warm-up blanket," Harmor concluded in his report. Harmor also found that one of the blanket samples "with a yellow-colored stain" – most likely part of the ejaculation – had DNA consistent with Sabrina's, though no intact spermatozoa could be detected in the sample. What likely was Sabrina's DNA was left through saliva, vaginal or other bodily secretion.

Suddenly, DNA, a forensics tool that did not even exist when John and Sabrina were killed, had put the prosecution's already wobbly case on the ropes. Henderson clung to the hope that his separate DNA tests – which took longer than expected because the lab he used did not have the necessary technology at hand – would yield a different result.

While he waited for the results, he forged ahead with his case in Sonoma

County, where he rented a house in anticipation of a long trial. Finally, after prosecuting the case solo, he was joined for the first time by a co-prosecutor, Nick Pohl.

Two juries were picked from some 1,050 prospective people who were questioned over 40 days. The prosecution's witness list alone included 100 names. TV stations and newspapers from all over Northern California put in media requests. Detailed exhibits and timelines were prepared. Courthouse employees in Santa Rosa worked for three months getting ready for what the preliminary hearing judge called "a once-in-a-lifetime case." The meter was running. Costs mounted.

And when the prosecution's DNA results finally came back on Jan. 26, 1993, David C. Henderson, district attorney for Yolo County since 1984, intrepid prosecutor of the Hunt party, the man who pursued the Hunt group after Sacramento passed, the guy who took Turner's word for it before, during and after the arrests, was royally screwed.

All because of four little semen stains that neither he nor anyone else could explain. Factoring in the three-year cost of his prosecution of the Hunt group (which was about $2 million when the case was dropped in 1993) by today's standards, it adds up to around $1 million per stain.

On Jan. 29, the juries, which took several weeks to select, were set to be sworn in. After swearing in, there would be no turning back under the double-jeopardy standard that holds defendants can't be prosecuted twice for the same offense. Henderson cut them off at the pass. "Your honor," Henderson intoned in his trademark low voice, which on this day, a low point in his career, he probably wished nobody could hear. "By a re-examination of certain items of evidence, we were able to determine that there were bodily fluids which evidenced a sexual assault which was contemporaneous with the abduction and murder of Sabrina Gonsalves and John Riggins."

Henderson added that he was sure the semen was from "a co-conspirator" and that he still had considerable evidence pointing to the Hunt group's guilt. But, he conceded, "the jury would not be able to find the defendants guilty beyond a reasonable doubt in light of the new evidence."

"I intend to move for a dismissal on that basis," he said.

Told by his attorneys before court that the charges would be dismissed, David Hunt, who rarely said much to anyone during his court appearances, who by all media accounts and courtroom gossip was a big baddie incapable of stringing a sentence together, wanted to address the court. Hunt's defense team was reluctant to let their client speak. After all, he was an uneducated career criminal. When charges are dropped, especially murder charges with the death penalty, it's best to just walk away, they told him. But Hunt persisted. He rose to address the court. His attorneys were surprised by his eloquence.

"It's very easy to make accusations against people, especially if you have the power of the government and the press behind you," Hunt said, glaring toward the prosecution table. "It's very hard to defend yourself, especially if you are a regular person like I am and my wife is.

"They say they have all this evidence. I say let them bring it. All I ever asked for since this case began was a chance to put this case before 12 honest people. This is a terrible thing that happened to these people, but it doesn't have anything to do with us. I want a trial. I have been in jail three years and three months with everyone in the world thinking I'm the bogeyman. I want a chance to say my side. How much longer must I go through this?"

Before sitting down, Hunt defended Suellen, saying that before her arrest she "had a job, a place to live, friends and a life."

"Now," Hunt noted, "she's about to be kicked out of jail with no clothes that fit her, her only crime being that she married me."

Once again, Thompson was in step with his "road dog." While he didn't offer a speech as impassioned as Hunt's, he, too, challenged Henderson to proceed with a trial.

Judge Keane responded to Henderson's motion to drop the charges with a dig at the prosecutor who had tried to disqualify him for sleeping. "To paraphrase T.S. Eliot, 'It is indeed a shame that this case ends not with a bang but a whimper.' "

A few days later Henderson also dropped the charges against Suellen and Lainer. Despite impending freedom, Lainer seethed; it got back to the judge that he wanted to "strike out" against Henderson. Before releasing him from custody, the judge warned Lainer that he would wind up back in jail if he retaliated. "Your Honor," Lainer countered, "I have been angry for three years. I have a right."

Judge Keane, who died not long after presiding over the case, denied a defense motion to dismiss the charges with prejudice. This left the possibility open that the Hunt group could still be prosecuted for the murders.

"I'm kind of in a daze, trying to resolve three years of involvement," Henderson glumly told a reporter as he left the courthouse in Santa Rosa.

24
Yin and Yang

Yolo County District Attorney David Henderson heard it from all sides. The judge. The defendants. Their attorneys. The media. Yolo County residents. Ending in a whimper. Millions spent on...what? Why didn't you test the blanket yourself before you filed charges? Why didn't you listen to Sacramento authorities when they told you the case was not winnable? Where was the evidence?

These were public criticisms. Privately, some wondered if Henderson didn't prosecute the case for political reasons as he ran for re-election, or if he wasn't in over his head: During all the pretrial maneuvering, he often had to take care of several children at night while his wife attended school, he challenged a drunken driving arrest that ended in a suspended jail sentence in 1991, and he continued to run the Yolo County District Attorney's Office.

Many familiar with the case told me they were surprised Henderson wasn't more skeptical of Turner's investigation.

"Fred would draw a conclusion early and then pursue it doggedly beyond all reason," said a former high-ranking Davis police officer who worked with Turner for several years. "Instead of being a collector of facts and adjusting his investigation based on what he collected, Fred would be blind to or ignore facts and information that did not support his theories. And he was always upbeat in where his investigations were going despite what was obvious to most others. We were flabbergasted that Dave Henderson filed (charges) when he did — but not surprised when the whole thing went south."

Turner also had his supporters at the Davis Police Department, including his chief, Vic Mentink. "I think he's one of the best detectives I ever had," Mentink said. "He's very thorough."

Perhaps Henderson fell prey to the "Prosecution Complex." Authors Thomas Frisbie and Randy Garrett coined this term in their insightful book, "Victims of Justice," in which three innocent men were arrested for the brutal murder of a 10-year-old Illinois girl. In this case, the authors illustrate how the prosecutors took such a myopic view of their case against the accused so as to ignore contradictory evidence that could possibly derail it.

> "The Prosecution Complex is most noticeable when an angry community is demanding justice," the authors note. "The Prosecution Complex encourages (prosecutors) to make deals with dubious snitches or suppress information that would help a defendant...Those suffering from the Prosecution Complex respond to community pressure rather than focusing on the facts."

In some ways, Henderson couldn't win for losing. Despite the criticisms, some believed Henderson pulled the plug too early, that he should have prosecuted the case, DNA be damned.

"In my heart I still feel we probably should have put the DNA aside and went on with the trial," Yolo investigator John Haynes said in 2001. "We may not have gotten a capital offense out of it, but life (in prison) for sure."

George Gonsalves even wrote a letter to the Woodland-based Daily Democrat newspaper supporting Henderson: "We appreciate the incredible effort and personal investment the DA's office has offered in this case...this system plays into the hands of the defense by permitting long delays and sanctioning the harassment of witnesses, all of which contributed to the release of these defendants."

Whether it was spin, desperation or an unwavering belief that he had the right culprits in the Hunt group, Henderson maintained after dropping the charges that he was not done with the case, that other leads were being pursued. Convinced there was a co-conspirator, Henderson had Fred Turner and Haynes chase down DNA samples from relatives and associates of the Hunt party, including Robert Coronado, whom they believed was with Lainer as he allegedly drove the Riggins van the day after the killings. Some 20 people were tested for DNA in the months after the charges were dropped. They were all excluded.

Other leads were checked from time to time, but by the mid-1990s, the case was once again cold, as if it had come full circle, and the circle was a perfect zero.

With DNA that didn't match the suspects, shaky eyewitness identifications eroded by time, a snitch whose motivations were suspect, and a complete lack of physical evidence, Henderson wisely cut his losses and dropped a case he should never have prosecuted without more evidence. After all, the guy he really wanted, Hunt, was already in federal prison serving a long sentence for the 1984 kidnapping of the Washington state couple. Henderson could have sat on the case pending more evidence. (Asked about this, Henderson said he took a now-or-never approach in 1989: he feared witnesses would die off or be hard to locate if he waited much longer to prosecute the Hunt group.)

With all the holes in the prosecution's case, including DNA that swiftly derailed it, you'd think there'd be an air of exoneration about the Hunt group. Wrong. Even DNA evidence didn't clear them in the eyes of many. There were several people who told me in 2000 and 2001 they were sure the Hunt quartet killed John and Sabrina — or believe they conspired with someone who did.

Chief among them was Sabrina's family when I interviewed them in Southern California in 2000. "They did it," Andrea Gonsalves said in her distinctive, hurried voice. "Oh, there's no question. The problem was the DNA was from someone else. There was a fifth guy...They planned it all; it was a big fun thing. In fact, they wanted to completely rape her, they wanted to do more. They wanted to keep her for a day or so. It didn't go well. They lost each other in the fog."

Other Gonsalves family members expressed similar sentiments. They said their suspicion only heightened when they viewed the suspects in court. Perhaps one of the Hunt party's big problems had to do with appearance: They certainly didn't play against type — at the least many thought they *looked* guilty. "These were bad people," said Kim Gonsalves, who even got a letter from a Thompson relative apologizing for Thompson's suspected role in the murders. "All you had to do is look at them to see that they were professional criminals."

(One of Sabrina's siblings did concede to me in 2001 when I expressed my doubts about the Hunt party that the family may have embraced the Hunt theory out of a desire for closure. "I think my parents may have believed whoever fed them the biggest line.")

It's a common sentiment. Everyone I talked to who went to the court appearances with any regularity said the same thing about the foursome: They did it. "Absolutely," maintained Phyllis Lipscomb, a close Riggins family friend who dutifully took notes on behalf of both families and attended as much as any spectator or reporter. In telling me this in 2000, she cited the $1,000 check to Doug Lainer, Katherine Bernard's testimony that she saw Lainer driving the Riggins van, and Hunt's "Is there anything I can do?" call to Gerald Gallego's mother-in-law, among other things.

Henderson, Turner and Haynes, whose combined recollection of key facts in the case often conflicted in interviews I did with each man, were adamant that they arrested the right people. While I expected Henderson and Turner to say as much, I wondered if Haynes, who was assigned to the case later and was likely less emotionally tied to it, remained convinced the Hunt group did it. "To my grave, they are the responsibles," insisted Haynes, who in making this statement in 2001 pointed to Rebecca Romani's so-called identifications of Hunt and Lainer at the Lucky shopping center and Katherine Bernard's ID of Lainer, among other things. (Haynes had less faith in snitch Lopez and derisively referred to him as a "worm.")

Longtime skeptics of the Hunt theory included John Riggins' parents, Ray Biondi and his detectives who investigated the case, evidence technician Faye Springer, and FBI profiler/former Davis police Detective Mark Safarik.

The Rigginses always had doubts, namely in the considerable logistics involved in coordinating four people of not a particularly high cunning or sobriety and pulling off an elaborate crime involving multiple locations in the blinding fog. "I really respect the people that investigated the Hunt group," Kate Riggins said in 2000. "I know the effort that went into it. The only thing is (the theory) is just so farfetched."

Biondi, who passed along the Hunt theory in the first place in the mid-1980s, long ago discounted it. "The murders appeared to be the work of a serial killer with a psychological motive known only to the killer in his own mind, based on fantasy." He told me in 2001 that the discovery of the semen on the blanket cemented his doubt. "Had this evidence been known earlier I might not have been so convinced of the Hunt lead, but at the time it was the only seemingly logical motive: copycat. Copycat crimes, however, are extremely rare. Now, with this evidence of a sexual assault, it is hard to imagine that this group somehow organized/pulled off this copycat crime and one of them assaulted Sabrina just to make it look good."

Biondi also pointed out something even some of Sabrina's family members had noted in expressing their suspicion of Hunt party guilt: Nobody rolled.

For more than three years the suspects were offered deals, threatened with the death penalty, badgered, cajoled, kept apart in jail, played one off the other. Nobody gave anybody else up. Of the 500-plus homicides he investigated, Biondi said he "never worked a murder case where this many people were involved and someone did not crack to save themselves."

Fred Turner in 2001 holds the bundle-up blanket in the Davis Police Department's evidence room. The semen stains were found (see the white square near the bottom of the frame) and removed from the blanket for DNA testing in 1992.

Joel Davis

Henderson countered that the suspects were "hardcore convict types." "They don't roll," he said.

While the blanket semen convinced Biondi and many others of the Hunt group's innocence, Turner for years had his own theory about it: It was planted. For whatever reason, the semen was not detected when Stan Reed and evidence technician Ken Mack handled and inspected the blanket, nor did Turner or the Sacramento County Crime Lab notice it in 1989. The blanket bounced around between the evidence rooms in Davis and Sacramento and was viewed more than once by defense attorneys and prosecution trial advocates. (When I saw it in 2001, it was wadded up unwrapped in a box in the Davis Police Department evidence room; I was free to handle it, though the stained portions had been long removed.) Turner told me on numerous occasions the semen either got on it via an evidence room tryst involving employees who had access to it or, more likely, was planted by someone in cahoots with the Hunt party, perhaps by a defense attorney or a defense team investigator who somehow acquired some semen from a third party.

This theory is farfetched. Most people I ran it by responded with raised eyebrows or outright laughs — and it does little to enhance Turner's credibility. But it bore consideration, especially in light of the shoddy, transitory way the evidence was handled. Though Faye Springer said the stains appeared old and that semen, one of the richest sources of DNA, could last for 12 years in a hot or cold storage room, the fact is nobody knows for certain when or how the semen got on the blanket. A tryst or a plant, therefore, cannot be ruled out (though later developments make it seem very unlikely).

And while Turner was pretty much alone in this theory — Henderson and Haynes did not discount it, but lacked Turner's enthusiasm — planting semen as a red herring in a criminal case is not unprecedented. In fact, there was a case involving both a copycat and planted semen just months before John and Sabrina were killed. Kenneth Bianchi, the so-called "Hillside Strangler" linked to 12 sex killings in Los Angeles and Washington state in 1978-79, was in jail for the murders when Veronica Compton, a wannabe playwright obsessed with murder and mutilation, began writing him fan letters. Seeing an alibi, Bianchi gave Compton a book with a rubber glove inside that contained his semen. He then ordered Compton to fly to Bellingham, Wash., and commit a copycat killing while planting the semen. Compton's attempt to kill a cocktail waitress failed, however. She was arrested, the ruse foiled.

In 1997, Anthony H. Turner, a serial rapist from Milwaukee convicted by DNA evidence, was incarcerated when another rape was reported in the same part of the city in which Turner committed his. Turner thus claimed a rapist responsible for all of the assaults was still at large and that he and the rapist shared the same DNA profile. Foster mailed some semen to an accomplice and paid her $50 to rub it on herself and claim she was the rape victim of another offender still at large. The ploy didn't work.

There have been other odd cases of planted DNA, including a Canadian doctor accused of raping patients, who initially duped DNA experts by implanting another man's blood in his arm to give as a sample. The point is that the evidence in the Riggins-Gonsalves case is its weakest link: between what was lost and what was never looked at after the murders occurred, there are countless scenarios that a savvy defense attorney will throw at a jury. The idea that the semen was planted didn't enter just Turner's head: Before the results came back, at least one defense attorney was prepared to imply that the prosecution planted the semen had the DNA profile not excluded his client.

"To say that we were all really paranoid about (the semen discovery) would be an understatement," recalled Lainer attorney Rod Beede. "I mean, you put three men in individual cells, and take their bed sheets out each week and you figure out what bodily fluids law enforcement might have access to and what they might do with them."

Among the many criticisms of Turner's investigation is that he lost his objectivity because he wanted to write a book on the case like the book Biondi wrote on the Gallego murders. Turner did entertain thoughts of writing a book – he even had a title, "No Apparent Motive." Whether it tainted his investigation is open to interpretation. The Hunt group is certain it did. "If Turner hadn't had his desires to write a book and Henderson hadn't had his desires to make sure his re-election looked good, none of this would have happened," Suellen said.

Beede also considered writing a book. He once asked Turner if he wanted to co-author a pro/con tome where Beede argued the Hunt group's innocence while Turner tried to prove their guilt.

After looking at this case for more than two years, I ultimately came to the opinion during the summer of 2002 that the Hunt group was likely innocent, a change from my initial reaction that they had some involvement. Doug Lainer's involvement seemed especially farfetched. I started becoming doubtful when I realized there was not a shred of physical evidence save perhaps a hair that in appearance matched Hunt's and was found on John's sweater, and Hunt and Lainer, often high, were not shrewd enough to get away with stealing sheets from a Holiday Inn yet were thought to be cunning enough to pull off an elaborate double homicide in the blinding fog with nothing save a few shaky witness identifications connecting them to it. Thompson was no sophisticate either; take Suellen out of the mix and add all the drugs, drinking and exhaustively long drives in a short time period and you're left with the Three Stooges.

"Knowing the cast of characters involved, I found it hard to believe that they could organize anything without something going to hell on it," Ray Biondi said.

If there was an epiphany for me, it came when my wife, Kelly, also a journalist, and I sat down with Lainer in the spring of 2002 in his modest Hayward apartment – and we both came away feeling he likely was being truthful. Lainer made an especially good point when I asked him about brazenly driving the Riggins van the day after the murders:

"Isn't that ludicrous?" he said, shaking his head. "Why would anybody drive around a van that two people were just killed in? Totally ludicrous."

25
Cold Hit

----

*"Once you cross police jurisdictions,
you have complicated the crime by a hundredfold."*

— Ray Biondi

A mostly forgotten mess.

That was the status of the Riggins-Gonsalves case when I started look-ing at it in the summer of 2000. Boxes upon boxes of case files gathered dust in Sonoma and Yolo courthouse basements known derisively as "tombs" or "dungeons." Court clerks seemed baffled or put out when asked to find them. I even drove to Sonoma County first because I was told — erroneously — by a Yolo clerk that the case files were all in Santa Rosa when in fact most of them were languishing in Woodland. To this day, it is not known for certain where all the evidence and case files are. "There have been a lot of hands in it," said one of the current Sacramento investigators working the case. And, it seemed, a lot of wayward thumbs.

After investigator John Haynes retired in 1996, Yolo County's active inves-tigation retired with him. While he seemed confident that he would refile charges after dropping them abruptly in 1993, Yolo DA Henderson told me in 2000 there was not much he could do with the case. "I have no place to go with it right now," he shrugged the one time I sat down with him at his office in Woodland (we traded many e-mails).

After Henderson dropped the charges, other names surfaced. Had the case gone to trial, the defense was set to float at least two alternate theories. One suggested the murders were committed by Benjamin Wai Silva and/or Joseph Shelton, who (see Chapter 13), brutally killed a young couple in Lassen County on Jan. 11, 1981. Shelton had ties to Sacramento, and was thought to be in the area the weekend John and Sabrina were slain. He and Silva were eliminated through DNA testing.

The other theory was that an employee of the Chandelier restaurant, the Lucky shopping center eatery where, by some accounts, John and Sabrina looked at a menu, was behind the murders. The employee, Marcus Felder,* had a criminal record, drove a van, lived within 3 miles of the body-recovery site, and was identified by at least one caller to The Bee's Secret Witness Program as the killer early in 1981. Yolo investigator Haynes said Felder was "looked at in-depth and cleared of any involvement."

Another chilling possibility that Kate Riggins wondered about for more than 20 years was that John and Sabrina were murdered by one of the most notorious and enigmatic killers in California history: the Zodiac. In the late 1960s, Northern California was intermittently terrorized by the Zodiac, a serial killer linked to at least six slayings, though in boastful letters to newspapers he claimed he killed as many as 37 people. The letters contained elaborate codes and threats of many more killings to come. The last letter known to definitely be from the Zodiac was sent to the San Francisco Chronicle in 1974.

In December 1981, around the one-year anniversary of John and Sabrina's deaths, the Rigginses received a letter with no return address. Thinking it was a cheerful holiday missive, Carrie Riggins opened it, only to recoil in horror at what it showed: Newspaper pictures of John and Sabrina had been pasted onto the letter, their names from the captions pasted over their throats. "I killed John & Sabrina," the typewritten letter reads. "Now I'm going to kill D.P. Pigs. Catch me if you can."

The letter also includes a code that was never deciphered: "D.W. A.R.E.P.J.A.S.W."

Authorities have analyzed the letter and stamp for fingerprints and/or DNA saliva, but reportedly found nothing. Most think it a cruel hoax. Kate Riggins to this day takes this letter seriously. She now doubts it is from the Zodiac but still believes it may have a role in the slayings.

Other intriguing possibilities emerged over time, but that's all they were: possibilities. In June 2001 highly regarded trace evidence expert Faye Springer, deadpan cool in a lab coat, told me at the Sacramento County Coroner's Office that if the case was going to be solved it would be through DNA. "The blanket was (new in its wrapping) when it went into the van," Springer said calmly. "When the bodies are found that blanket is ripped out of the wrapping. So it would have to have been used — and it's not John Riggins' semen. So logic tells you it has to be your crook."

Anne Marie Schubert
Sacramento Bee

Mindful of this, and not particularly taken with Fred Turner's plant theory, I periodically pressed Henderson and the California Department of Justice — which was said to have the DNA samples from the comforter — for information regarding the DNA. And I had trouble getting clear answers. There was enough stonewalling that at one point I discussed with the Rigginses the possibility of using some of the reward money still being held in the case to have a private DNA expert with connections in law enforcement retest the DNA and try and find a match.

On June 19, 2002, I brought the case to the attention of Sacramento County prosecutor Anne Marie Schubert, who, after talking with Kate Riggins, became very interested in the double-homicide. Schubert is a bright, wiry blonde who oversees her unit's cold-hit DNA match program and whose late father, coincidentally, was an orthopedic surgeon who knew Dick Riggins. I contacted her immediately after learning of her role in the DNA-related arrest of a Ronald Porter, 41, in the 1983 murder of Teresa Hightower, 23, a Sacramento State student who was found in her downtown Sacramento apartment bound, her throat stabbed. The arrest was made with the help of a state grant for counties that could use DNA from unsolved homicides involving sexual assault. The Riggins-Gonsalves case seemed an ideal candidate for this new program. At the least I wanted to know if there was a link between the Hightower murder and the Davis couple. And to Schubert's credit, she pursued it doggedly after I gave her the heads-up.

She and I traded information (she got the better part of the trades: I would not want to play poker with Anne Marie Schubert, or anybody from the Sacramento District Attorney's Office, for that matter) about the case throughout the summer of 2002. I faxed and e-mailed her photos, the FBI profile and other key details. At first she focused on the Abbott theory.

The Abbott theory (see Chapter 13) surfaced early in 1981 through the late Davis Detective Bob Persons. The theory was that John Gordon Abbott, 25, killed John and Sabrina to avenge his younger brother Michael's death after the two brothers robbed a Davis jewelry store in 1976. Michael was killed by a blast from a Davis police officer's shotgun after he and his brother burglarized the Gold Lion jewelry store at night and set off an alarm.

John Riggins was the Abbotts' paperboy, and resembled Michael Abbott. Also, on the night John and Sabrina were kidnapped after leaving the Veterans Memorial, there was a five-year reunion for Michael Abbott's Davis High class in an adjoining room.

John Abbott was in jail on Dec. 20, 1980, in Trail, British Columbia, on charges stemming from his involvement in a Nov. 24, 1980, shootout with Royal Canadian Mounties in which an associate, John Hennessey, 23, was killed. He was not even in the same country as John and Sabrina the night they were abducted. But he was in British Columbia before and when the murders occurred — and the matchbook in the van came from British Columbia. Authorities once thought it possible that he could have ordered an acquaintance in the Bay Area, Phillip Thompson, a criminal with a record of violence, including murder, to kill John and Sabrina. Abbott's trail cooled after detectives interviewed Thompson and could find nothing to connect either man to the killings. However, Schubert was very interested in the matchbook and how it got from British Columbia to Riggins' van. "There's got to be a reason it's in the van," she said.

Then, on Aug. 27, 2002, the would-haves, could-haves and other speculation gave way to cold, calculating science. Like a delayed sonic boom that took more than 21 years to strike, a DNA "cold hit" was made on the blanket semen sample after the semen DNA was retyped and compared to DNA from a national database — in this case, DNA from Washington state sex offenders.

And the name was someone nobody had ever heard of, a convicted sex offender who despite the hundreds of tips, dozens of suspects and myriad investigations in this case flew under the radar for more than two decades:

Richard Joseph Hirschfield. AKA *"Who the Hell," "Come Again," "Damn,"* and *"Huh?"*

Hirschfield, 53 when the hit was made, is a convicted child molester. At the time of the match he was in prison in Washington state until at least May 2010. His name was never associated with the case. But in addition to a DNA match said to be something as precise as one in 240 trillion, he has a criminal past that fits, if indeed the murders were a sex crime, which now seems certain.

Hirschfield has a home-invasion rape conviction from the mid-1970s in Mountain View, Calif. where he easily controlled a couple and another girl. He was released from a prison not far from Davis the summer before John and Sabrina were killed. And though mostly a drifter, he possibly worked in Davis as a heating and air-conditioner repairman around the time of the murders. Perhaps, authorities surmise, he got the idea to assault and kill Sabrina after seeing her during a repair job at her condo or a neighboring one. (Long before Hirschfield was a suspect, Andrea Gonsalves told me that on one occasion in 1980 a man "waved a tool around" at the condo and Sabrina's German shepherd lunged at him.)

Hirschfield also seemed a fairly close match to an eyewitness sighting that got lost or was ignored in Yolo's prosecution of the Hunt group. Shortly after John and Sabrina were killed, a motorist told authorities she saw a man near the ravine where the bodies were found about 9 a.m. on Dec. 21, 1980, the morning after they were kidnapped. The man wore a yellow, blood-stained T-shirt and a "drab, Army-style jacket." He was described as white, stocky, between 22 and 26, up to about 6 feet 2 inches tall with shaggy or feathered hair parted down the middle. (See police sketch, Chapter 12.) In December 1980, Hirschfield, who is 6 feet tall, was 31 and stocky. A prison mugshot taken that year shows he had shaggy hair parted down the middle. He wore an Army-style jacket both at the Mountain View rape and when he was arrested in nearby Sunnyvale.

Ray Biondi said in 1981 that the witness saw the man emerge from some bushes along the highway and enter a dark-brown standard-size pickup truck. "It appeared he was waiting for this particular vehicle, according to the witness," Biondi said. "The vehicle came and he just got right in."

A second white male adult drove the pickup, which suggests that the killer had an accomplice.

Hirschfield, in fact, seems a close match to the FBI profile done on the case in 1983; more so than Hunt, anyway. Said to be highly intelligent if a bit odd, Hirschfield is described by Sacramento Homicide Bureau Supervisor Craig

Hill as "Unabomber smart." Hirschfield denied any involvement with the murders and immediately asked for an attorney when Sacramento County detectives in November 2002 confronted him with the new evidence in his jail cell at the McNeil Island Corrections Center in Washington state.

"He's pretty sharp," Hill said. "Once he knew that we were from Sacramento I think he put two and two together. There was a little dialogue, just BS-ing. But once it came down to DNA he said, 'You know what, I'd rather just talk to an attorney.' "

There was no attempt to induce a confession via an informant, because, Hill said, it would have involved difficult logistics. "That far away we don't know the prison officials, we don't know who we can trust in that location. So rather than trying that type of thing we decided to go for (the confrontation) because we had his DNA."

The cold hit triggered hot emotions. When the calculating science from the DNA mixed with human nature, all hell broke loose. For starters, I went from ally to foe, from the chronicler of a long-dormant mystery to the interloper in a hot investigation.

Although both families and cold-hit prosecutor Schubert credited this book project with getting the case reopened, I was seen as a potential liability. Schubert and the two new Sacramento County detectives assigned to the case, in a private meeting with the families in Southern California in early September 2002 (Schubert even asked me for the Gonsalveses' phone number prior to the meeting), decided to keep the news of the cold hit from me, to let me publish this book (originally due for a December 2002 release) without filling me in, which was certainly their prerogative.

And it was my prerogative to continue reporting. Which I did, cautiously, and, for some three months, without doing much besides contacting "official sources." I stayed away from Hirschfield and anyone connected to him. A source tipped me off to this seismic development in October of 2002. "Hold off on going to the publisher," the source said. "Hint: DNA."

My knowledge of this new information did not sit well with anybody, particularly the new investigation team. To make a long story short, after some heated inquires to Schubert where I told her flat-out that I felt she had used me, I was "invited" to downtown Sacramento on Oct. 17, 2002, to discuss the case with her, John O'Mara (the Sacramento County prosecutor who originally passed on the case), the two current detectives assigned to the case, and Hill. This meeting — five professional interrogators and me — did not go well.

.

It seemed obvious that the point of the "meet and browbeat" as I came to call it, was to intimidate me off the story, something I strongly suspect would not have happened had I been a big-name author or with a major media organization. I was a mom-and-pop operation at best in shaky health (literally shaky, having been diagnosed with Parkinson's by this time) to boot, and they knew it. I took the following month off, and thanks to some reporting tricks and dumb luck, confirmed Hirschfield's name, of all places on Classmates.com (*Richard Hirschfield: E-mail me! Ask me to build a profile!*).

And in perhaps the most surreal moment of this strange twist to the case, the Sacramento County investigative team sent a U-Haul trailer over to Woodland and had Henderson hand over the dozens of boxes of case files. Saying they wanted an unbiased look at the case with fresh eyes, the new team, suspicious of outsiders, did not want Yolo's help, they did not want my help, they did not want Ray Biondi's help. "I worked on this case for over 10 years and nobody's bothered to contact me," a jilted Biondi said after the DNA match was made.

Though apparently frozen out, Haynes and Turner did not stay idle. Long convinced that there was a fifth suspect who aided the Hunt party and eluded detection, the two Yolo detectives, now both retired but anxious to jump back into a case that consumed years of their lives, launched an unofficial counter-investigation. For a time I was a sort of middleman, relaying information between the two counties. They did not want to communicate directly with one another, and, like competing media organizations, still don't. Something Biondi told me over lunch in 2001 suddenly seemed profound. Whether intentional or not, perhaps the smartest thing the killer(s) did was involve two counties with two sets of egos, agendas and theories. "Once you cross police jurisdictions," Biondi said, "you have complicated the crime by a hundred-fold, because police now have to coordinate their efforts."

While the Sacramento team told me during the few discussions I had with them following our meeting that they could find no ties to the Hunt party, Yolo remained convinced Hirschfield was the long-sought fifth person – this despite the fact that dozens of Hunt associates had already been checked out and some two dozen had given DNA samples. When Hunt kidnapped the young Washington couple in 1984, there was a white man named "Scooter" who was peripherally involved but never identified. Turner and Haynes believed Scooter could be Richard Hirschfield, that he was a partner in Hunt's alleged marijuana business in the Pacific Northwest.

"With regard to Hirschfield," Henderson noted in a Dec. 2, 2002, e-mail, "my thought is that he is the final piece of the puzzle that makes it all work. Each bit of information that we develop shows a parallel track with potential contact points at the critical times...Consider the effort that Hunt, et. al, put into trying to disguise their locations and activities. Their guile is impressive and we certainly don't believe that we have insight into most of their methods. We had always assumed that Lainer was the 'mule' to connect with the unidentified accomplice. Fred and John had turned over every known rock to ID this other party and we always believed that there was one piece missing."

E-mails from Turner and Haynes expressed a similar sentiment:

Turner: Sacramento "is not interested in finding any connection between (Hirschfield) and Hunt, et al; we're willing to see if there is a connection, and believe that there may well be one, greatly simplifying prosecution of all suspects."

Haynes, who doesn't mince words, was characteristically blunt and to the point in his all-caps missive: "I'M TELLIN YOU...HUNT, HUNT, HUNT 'N THOMPSON, THOMPSON, THOMPSON. THE DNA DUDE WAS JUST A SHILL......."

The Yolo team had a point: Hirschfield and Hunt *did* have some things in common.

Most compelling was the fact that both men were apparently in the Santa Clara County Jail in 1975 and the California Medical Facility in Vacaville, the latter apparently at the same time, albeit briefly. Not only that, but both men had ties to Oregon and Washington as well as Sacramento. Not only that, but Hunt and Hirschfield were paroled to San Mateo County in 1980 — Hirschfield in July and Hunt in October. Hunt had relatives in Chico, Calif., Hirschfield grew up not far from there. Throw in Suellen and Lainer's ties to San Mateo County during this period, and the Hunt theory again had legs.

And just as they figured a decade earlier with the discovery of the DNA, Henderson, Haynes and Turner were excited that they'd found the proverbial smoking gun. But in perhaps the final blow to a theory that seems little more than, well, a theory (albeit a compelling one with some very odd coincidences), the Hunt-Hirschfield link simply would not pan out.

And then Joker Joe entered the picture and pushed Hunt off the stage.

26
Hirschfield

A fter the DNA match was made, authorities probed Richard Hirschfield's ties to the Davis-Sacramento area, mainly through his family, which has long had a history in Colusa County, specifically the town of Arbuckle, which is as rural it sounds.

What they found is likely the final piece of the puzzle. When John and Sabrina were killed, one of Hirschfield's younger brothers, Joe Hirschfield, 25, was probably living in or had just vacated the Centennial Estates mobile home park in Rancho Cordova — about 7 miles west of the ravine where John and Sabrina were found and just off Folsom Boulevard. Joe's home on Lord Street was on the way to the ravine from Davis. At the time of the murders he was a Mather Air Force Base mechanic who had a wife, Sally,* and two small children, but was separated and living by himself, perhaps in the mobile home. It is believed that Joe gave Richard a place to stay after he was released from prison in July 1980. Joe also worked prior to the slayings as a mechanic/attendant at a Fair Oaks service station, where the station owner, Cecil Thixton, remembers him as an "honest, good employee."

He definitely knew the area.

After almost 22 years, the mystery seemed less mysterious. Authorities now speculate that Richard Hirschfield, who apparently didn't have a car at the time, snatched John and Sabrina in Davis in John's van and then drove them or had them drive to his younger brother's home.

"A possibility is Richard did this abduction, drove out to Rancho Cordova and said, 'Hey brother look what I got,'" Sacramento County Homicide Bureau Supervisor Sgt. Craig Hill noted. "And then Joe ended up picking Richard up" near the ravine the next morning.

And it now appears the murders were grislier than originally thought. With the Hunt theory, Ray Lopez's testimony and the window of opportunity suggested that Sabrina and John were held captive for a relatively short period of time and Sabrina was not raped. Now it seems certain that Sabrina

Richard Hirschfield in high school, left; in prison in California in 1980; and in prison in Washington state.

was raped, likely by two men, and perhaps held overnight along with John, who may have been forced to watch as part of some sort of sadistic control fantasy. This may also explain Sabrina's underwear being inside out, and the suspected semen stains in them: If she was held overnight, possibly at Joe's secluded residence — Lord Street is tucked away at the south end of the trailer park and, like Sabrina's condo, isolated and dark at night — there would have been time to redress her. No wonder John fought back; no wonder he went down swinging.

It gets worse. If the Hirschfield brothers slit the sweethearts' throats, they had training: both apprenticed as butchers on a relative's farm growing up in Colusa County, Hill said.

In mid-November 2002, Joe worked as a highly regarded journeyman mechanic at Kuni Cadillac in Beaverton, Ore. He had lived in Oregon since 1983, perhaps out of a desire to live in anonymity. While there was nothing more than geography and a sibling connecting him to the murders during this stage of the investigation, Joker Joe must have figured the authorities knew more than they did. Either that or his conscience simply got the best of him. In any event, Joe, known to be a terrible liar (one of his ex-wives said he couldn't even get away with cheating at a game of spades without sweating and fidgeting), nervously cooperated with Sacramento detectives, telling them — perhaps to simply take the heat off — that he believed his older brother lived and worked in Davis the weekend of the murders.

When told of the DNA match, Joe began to tremble. Still, the authorities had nothing on him.

Joe Hirschfield clowning during a boat trip, left. Right, the honeymoon car in
which he also killed himself.

Lana Hirschfield

The following morning, he killed himself in his car in his big barn, leaving a two-page note that is both damning and frustratingly vague. In it, he
expresses his love for his wife, and that he had been living in horror for 20
years. He admitted being present during the murders, but that Richard committed them. He added that he expected the detectives to return and that "It
is only a matter of time before they find my DNA, too" — but little else.

The note, said Hill, is "a little confusing."

"I wish the bastard would have told us what he did."

Lana Hirschfield, Joe's third and final wife, met her husband during a
scuba diving trip in the late 1990s and adored him ("we never so much as
had an argument"). She had no idea he had such a dark secret in his past.
She said Joe rarely mentioned Richard or his family. She did not know his
oldest brother was even in prison in Washington on the molest charge. Lana
did ask her husband before he went to bed the final night of his life about
the detectives showing up at her door. Joe mentioned that he took in Richard after Richard got out of prison in 1980.

Joe, Lana said, "definitely was distraught because of his brother being in
prison again and potentially being in (new) trouble on top of it. We did not
talk about it much at all because as far as I was concerned, it really didn't
have anything to do with us and I didn't know any of his family anyway. I
was working late that night so we didn't have much time before we went to
sleep." Lana added: "you could have knocked me over with a feather" upon
learning of Joe's suspected involvement, and believes he killed himself out of
shame. "I don't think he wanted to face me," she said, adding that the suicide

note addressed to her doesn't say much. "It's really very vague," she sighed. "There really isn't much there."

That leaves Richard. And Richard, who showed little emotion when told of his brother's suicide, is, so far, not talking. He may never.

Unlike David Hunt, Richard Joseph Hirschfield isn't ferocious looking. He's rather sorrowful in appearance. With his droopy eyes, stringy hair, unkempt beard, thick build and lazy stare, he looks like something out of a ZZ Top video gone wrong. He lacks David Hunt's flinty gaze, swagger and muscular build. His family wrote him off years ago — he has few if any visitors since being locked up for child molestation in 1997. He sat in his jail cell in Washington after the match in pathetic isolation, whiling his days away writing in journals, much of it, Hill said, fantasizing about young girls.

But there are similarities. Like Hunt, Richard Hirschfield does have a rather pronounced, bulbous nose. He is also the same race and size as Hunt, shares a similar hair color and is close in age (Hunt was born in 1944, Hirschfield in 1949). Take away the shaky alleged sightings of Doug Lainer the weekend of the killings — Richard Thompson and Suellen were never identified as being in Sacramento — and you are left only with shaky alleged sightings of Hunt. Perhaps witnesses who believe they saw Hunt confused him with Hirschfield. Maybe, just maybe, it all comes down to confusion in the fog, and the striking similarity of the bulbous nose.

And Henderson, Haynes and Turner were right on one count: It appears the murders were indeed the work of a copycat. But not a copy of Gerald Gallego. Richard Hirschfield, if he did them, copied himself (though there is some speculation that he was aware of the November 1980 Arden Fair kidnapping/murders and perhaps "got an idea" after media accounts of the killings or Gallego's arrest). There are some ominous similarities between the Davis murders and the rape for which Hirschfield was arrested in 1975.

At 8:30 p.m. on April 30, 1975, Richard Hirschfield broke into an apartment in Mountain View, startling two sisters, ages 21 and 16, and the younger sister's boyfriend. He wore gloves, his bushy face distorted and disguised by a pair of women's nylons. In an Army-style jacket he packed a .38-caliber revolver equipped with a homemade silencer. Entering through the kitchen he said, "Freeze!" adding, "I want bread. Nobody will be hurt."

But it wasn't just money he was after. After searching the frightened trio, he ordered them on the floor, where he swiftly bound them with a new rope he had with him, deftly slicing the lengths with a knife that was part of his arsenal. He tied the hands and feet of the boyfriend and the older sister. He left the younger sister's legs free, then placed her on her back and unzipped her pants and put his hand down them.

When the terrified girl cried out, Richard removed his hand and announced, "Who wants to be raped?"

The older sister, in an incredible act of bravery and self-sacrifice, said, "You can rape me. All I ask is that you not do it in front of the other two."

"OK," Richard replied. "I may be bad but I have morals."

He carried the other two, still bound by rope, into a bedroom, then returned to the front room, where he held the revolver to the older sister's head.

"Suck my — ," he demanded.

The woman complied, but soon gagged and stopped. "I'm gonna get sick."

"OK, then get on the floor," Richard countered. He forced the woman to have intercourse.

Richard then returned to the bedroom and ordered the young couple to take off their clothes, again fondling the younger sister. "Get in the closet and stay there," he said.

The burly intruder marched into the kitchen, where he dumped the girls' purses on a table, scavenging for money. He also searched the cupboards and rattled a piggybank. Before exiting, he sliced the phone line with the knife, leaving his victims stunned, naked and with no means of quick communication.

There were chilling similarities between this rape and the Riggins-Gonsalves slayings, namely in how the victims (including a male) were controlled, how the females' legs were left unbound so as to have access to their pelvic areas, and — this is perhaps the most telling similarity — how personal effects were fiendishly rifled after the attacks were carried out. In the apartment it was purses, in the Riggins van it was presents.

The big difference, of course, was that in one case the victims were killed. It is also worth noting that the 1983 FBI profile done on the Davis slayings mentioned that the killer may have felt no choice but to kill John and Sabrina because Sabrina may have lost consciousness after being bound with the tape. I'm inclined to believe it had at least as much to do with Sabrina's morals and stubbornness and John fighting for her.

Ten days after the 1975 Mountain View apartment rape, a patrolman noticed Richard loitering in a Sunnyvale apartment complex at night, and noted he matched the description of the Mountain View rapist. He wore a similar coat and had a nylon mask in his pocket.

On the seat of Richard's car was a note indicating he perhaps intended to rape again. It read "sexy chick" with a woman's address about a mile away. Found in Hirschfield's car were the revolver and homemade silencer, gunpowder, three homemade bombs and several keys to apartments and vehicles. Also found was a garrote, a strangling device fashioned out of piano wire and wood handles. While he didn't use the garrote in the Mountain View rape, it was significant here because John and Sabrina had possible ligature or teasing and/or "hesitation" marks on their necks, according to their autopsies. (Sabrina also wore a tie that perhaps was tightened to control her.)

Hirschfield was tried for the Mountain View rape/robbery in September 1975. He pleaded not guilty by reason of insanity. He was found guilty and sane — though the jury and court-appointed psychiatrists noted he needed psychiatric care — and sentenced to state prison. Because it was his first major offense, he got a fairly light sentence, and served less than five years at the California Medical Facility in Vacaville — about 30 miles west of Davis. He was released from prison on July 2, 1980, and, in 1981, registered as a convicted sex offender in Williams, Calif., about 50 miles from Davis.

According to court records, Richard is the oldest child of a "very chaotic family." The Hirschfields were poor and moved a lot in Richard's youth. Richard's mother, a cook at a convalescent hospital, gave birth to him when she was 15. His father, who died of complications from alcoholism, abandoned the family when Richard was in third grade, though his mother remarried. As a teen, Richard stole things and got in fights on dares to prove himself; at one point he was placed in an uncle's custody as a ward of the court and even attended parochial school. He graduated from Colusa High School in 1967, then headed to the Bay Area and even enrolled for a time in College of San Mateo, though a lack of money and focus kept him from pursuing a degree. Described by some as brilliant, he had a thirst for knowledge so intense that he would ask college friends if he could attend classes on their behalf just to soak up information that he otherwise could not afford. He also studied chemistry and electronics, perhaps because he was said to be interested in bombs and weapons.

Richard smoked heavily, dabbled in drugs (including sniffing gasoline) and had problems with alcohol. But the addiction that seemingly led him on the path of ruin was his addiction to Beth.

Richard met Beth in 1969. The romance blossomed, and the couple soon moved in together. Beth's father even helped get Richard, who also worked as a grocery clerk and a truck driver, a job as a sheetmetal worker. But she seemed lukewarm about the relationship. In December 1972, she refused Richard's marriage proposal. In 1974, Beth, fresh out of college, took a job with the Internal Revenue Service. During a business trip, she became involved with another IRS employee, an agent in Witchita, Kan.

This is when Richard's world unraveled. When Beth, described as "gorgeous" by investigators, tried to end the relationship in 1974, Richard had a meltdown and began threatening both Beth and her new lover. This perhaps explains the homemade bombs: Richard not only wanted to kill the other man, he planned to blow him up, court records show. Court records also show that Richard threatened to rape Beth when she refused to have sex with him and that he felt inadequate in his inability to bring her to orgasm.

One psychiatrist suggested Richard committed the 1975 rape to avenge losing Beth to another man: "He firmly believes that the (victim) was a substitute for his girlfriend and that the anger associated with his actions was his way of hurting the girlfriend," the psychiatrist noted. "There was tremendous tension during the interview when talking about his ex-girlfriend: Tears come to his eyes, he began rapid breathing, clenching and opening his fists. His belief that his ex-girlfriend can help him and that he needs her to function in his life is almost delusional...His intention to waste any man who might stand in the way of their relationship is still very strong in his mind...A lifelong sense of sexual inadequacy permeates his mind."

The inability to perform sexually may explain why Sabrina was not raped in a "conventional" way.

"I have theories," Sacramento Detective Stan Reed said long before the DNA match, when he expressed serious doubts about Hunt's involvement while having some choice words for Yolo DA Henderson. "And the theory was that Sabrina was going to be the victim. And the guy that did it was an inadequate sex offender unable to maintain an erection, which would account for the fondling, the scratching, the panties inside out. He jerked off on the blanket, or she was forced to provide him with oral sex and he ejaculated. There's just a whole lot of things" it could have been.

(Reed was at least partially correct: After the DNA match was made, Sabrina's oral slides were recovered and retested. They tested positive for semen that could not be typed. She therefore likely was forced to provide oral sex to her abductors.)

The prosecutor in the 1975 rape case described Richard as an "extremely intelligent, highly energetic, dangerous individual." Joe Hirschfield's first wife, Sally, once visited Richard in prison in Vacaville and said Richard bragged about playing dumb. "I remember him saying how he was going to counselors who were trying to figure him out. And he would tell them whatever he thought they wanted to hear. He would lie. He would try to manipulate all the tests they would have him do."

Joe's involvement has everyone who knew him puzzled; he was well-liked and respected by many, particularly for his work ethic. However, he was, according to a woman he had a relationship with, persistent when he wanted sex. "There were no restraints or anything kinky, but I never really felt like I was allowed to say no," she said. "And many times I would wake up in the middle of the night with him on me. Now that I am older and wiser I can see that that was strange...He forced it once."

Sally, who married Joe in Reno when she was 15 and he was 18, has few fond memories of their marriage. She said Joe had girlfriends on the side and failed to pay child support for many years after they divorced in the early 1980s. But she also described him as a hard worker, good provider and a fun-loving guy, and she cannot believe he would be involved in a double-homicide. "I cannot come up with a scenario that makes any sense to me of how he would be in the situation he was in. I'm totally shocked and can't imagine what happened for him to be in it."

Like Lana Hirschfield, Sally doubts Joe had any connection to the Hunt party. "I really don't think anybody else had any part of it. I think Joe got wrapped up in something and possibly was scared to tell the truth and it shows by him killing himself — he didn't want to deal with it. He'd have to admit his part, even if it was just rape; that was still bad enough. If he's going to kill himself why not tell everything? I think he was probably afraid of Richard."

After the slayings, Joe and Richard lived in a home in the Colusa County town of Arbuckle. According to Sally, Richard moved out of the Arbuckle home sometime in 1981 and Joe stuck around until 1983, when he moved to Oregon.

Little seems to be known about Richard Hirschfield's life between 1981 and his Washington state child molest in 1996, though in 1983 he was arrested, but apparently never charged, for brandishing a weapon in the small Northern California community of Willows. He did, however, live in Arcata on California's remote North Coast in 1992 (ironically enough, so did I, apparently for a time in the same neighborhood). His arrest record is clean from 1983 until 1996, though the Department of Justice is investigating whether he is involved in other crimes. Run a credit check on him and you will come up blank save a bankruptcy in the late 1990s. Detectives have had a hard time tracing his path, though there is some speculation that he may have been drawn to the Davis of 1980 because it had several now-gone working-class bars downtown, a university, and even the Westlane X-rated drive-in theater — all potential draws for rural outsiders looking for action on a Saturday night. He might still be at large if not for his affinity for little girls.

On July 28, 1996, court records show, Richard lived in Snohomish, Wash., an idyllic community 30 miles north of Seattle and close to Vancouver, British Columbia. He worked as a draftsman and had a girlfriend. They were swimming at the Aqua Barn Ranch, a public pool in King County, Wash. "Hi, I'm Rick," he would tell the excited children, who flocked to the furry bear of a man described as having a big scar on his back. "Want me to toss you in the air? It'll be fun."

Two girls, ages 9 and 11, took him up on the offer. As the children splashed around him, he took one of the girls into the crook of his arm. But instead of instantly throwing her in the air, he reached under her one-piece bathing suit and fondled her vagina. Before the girl said anything, he removed his hand and said, "Sorry." He later fondled her a second time.

Richard molested the second girl in a similar fashion. He was arrested when the girls' mothers compared stories and called the authorities, who believe there were other young girls who fell prey to the friendly man in the pool.

In June 1997, he agreed to plead guilty to one felony count each of child molestation and rape of a child. He was sent to McNeil Island Correction Facility near Seattle until at least 2010, where he apparently had a TV in his cell and Internet access, among other prison "perks." He was moved to Clallam Bay Corrections Center, Washington state's tightest-security facility, after the DNA match. His presentencing report noted that he is suspected of other sex crimes.

Authorities investigating the Riggins-Gonsalves murders are, somewhat understandably, tight-lipped about the case. I gleaned most of my information through public documents and interviews with the few people willing to talk about it. Given the bizarre history of the blanket, they are looking for corroborating evidence on Richard and Joseph Hirschfield: New DNA technology may allow the degraded semen in Sabrina's panties to be typed. The

68 fingerprints found in the van are being checked, though Richard wore gloves in his 1975 rape and robbery. Before Joe's wife had him cremated (there was no service for months so as to keep Joe's suicide a secret), DNA and fingerprint samples were taken from him. A fingerprint or some other evidence tying either man to the crime in addition to the blanket DNA would be a tremendous boost to the prosecution as the defense will likely pounce on the blanket's strange, almost pathetic history and Turner's planted evidence theory. In conversations with Sacramento prosecutors John O'Mara and Anne Marie Schubert in late 2003 and early 2004, I learned that in addition to the oral slide from Sabrina's rape kit testing positive for semen (I learned this, in fact, before Sabrina's family, which added to a schism in this case between the DA's office and sheriff's investigators since the DNA match). One of the blanket stains was possibly Joe's semen, though typing it may be difficult because he had had a vasectomy. O'Mara said lab tests were not conclusive. "There is stuff you could read into the results that would include him but there is nothing definitive," he said.

The one piece of non-DNA evidence left behind in the van that appears to tie the Hirschfields to the crime is the matchbook from British Columbia. Both brothers smoked. One possibility: Authorities believe Joseph may have picked it up during a scuba diving trip in Vancouver, but both Lana Hirschfield and Joe's first wife, Sally, say he did not take up the sport until well after 1980.

Despite the DNA, despite Richard Hirschfield having a history of sex crimes, prosecuting him will be a challenge given that the murders occurred in 1980, and evidence handling was shoddy at best. He could be offered a deal, perhaps life without parole in exchange for telling what he knows about what happened on Dec. 20, 1980. Charging him with the death penalty adds considerable time and expense to the case, which at this writing, is stuck in the arraignment phase – his first half-dozen court appearances were simply continued while attorneys on both sides look to curb outrageous costs such as how to copy a staggering 150,000 pages of discovery going back a quarter of a century.

Justice Waits...for Kinko's.

Because it is a death penalty charge on a cold case, Hirschfield gets three attorneys – one of them a DNA specialist – and an automatic appeal if found guilty. Both John and Sabrina's families favor the death penalty and are wary of any deals. "We're willing to wait," George Gonsalves has said. The wait may be long if the defense embraces what Sacramento refers to as a ready-made defense theory: Yolo's dogged prosecution of the Hunt group.

"My opinion is this was a sexually motivated homicide and all along I didn't think much of the (Hunt theory)," Sacramento prosecutor Schubert said.

But Hirschfield's defense is likely to embrace it. Schubert knows this, and more than once hinted that her office's biggest obstacle would be impeaching the Hunt theory, or as she likes to put it:

"The defense calls Fred Turner."

Joel Davis

Hirschfield

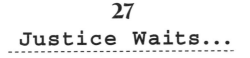

27
Justice Waits...

When the cold hit was made, and the case appeared to be solved at long last — though if there's a lesson to be learned in this story it's that nothing is certain — I was asked if I would change the title of this book.

But justice waits...Richard Hirschfield, who likes to play games, likes to fire his attorneys and in the view of some, likes to feign mental incapacity, will likely ensure that. After a two-year post-DNA-match investigation that apparently yielded little additional evidence or witnesses connecting him to the Davis murders, he was publicly named as a suspect by The Davis Enterprise in June 2004 after frustrated investigators were unable to place him in Davis. They finally sought the public's help, something that in hindsight they probably should have done much sooner. And with Hirschfield already in custody in Washington, new homicides in Sacramento routinely pushed the investigation to the bottom of the deck in a city that never seems to have a shortage of fresh slayings.

It was also in June 2004 that a warrant was issued for Hirschfield's arrest, a warrant overseen by Sacramento prosecutor John O'Mara that includes Yolo's Hunt theory ("I did not want it to appear that we were not telling the judge the whole story," O'Mara would later say). Hirschfield unsuccessfully fought extradition to Sacramento from Washington state based on sovereignty theories popular with rural constitutionalists — at one point he reportedly denied he was Richard Hirschfield because his name was spelled in all-caps on court documents.

Hirschfield was arrested on Sept. 25, 2004, to a brief but intense media frenzy and additional communication breakdowns that have been an unfortunate hallmark of this case. Investigators were hoping to finally get some time alone with him during his extradition to California to ask some pressing questions, but even this plan went astray because of scheduling confusion and/or objections from defense attorneys during the weekend extradition.

Hirschfield's first court appearance, one of many in which he asked for

Richard Hirschfield with attorney Linda Parisi at his arraignment. (He wore dark glasses after a jailhouse fight.)

Davis Enterprise

a continuance rather than enter a plea, was attended by Sabrina's parents, who were poised and even managed to smile a few times.

It was at this first appearance that Hirschfield was apparently charged with raping John as well as Sabrina — a new, disturbing detail and something widely reported on the evening news; at least two channels showed a distraught cousin of John's talking about how upsetting it was to learn he had also been sexually assaulted. The complaint as read by the judge certainly sounded as if John was sexually assaulted, but it was later announced that the charge concerns John's murder being committed during Sabrina's rape. Oops.

Bearded and unkempt, Hirschfield wore dark sunglasses at the hearing because he got pummeled by prisoners for demanding to use a jailhouse payphone out of turn. He is now being kept in his own cell for his own protection.

Justice certainly waits for the Hunt party if they are indeed innocent, which seems certain, albeit with some interesting recent developments involving David Hunt. While there are some strange time/location coincidences link-

George Gonsalves speaks to the media as Sheriff's Homicide Bureau Supervisor Sgt. Craig Hill listens in the background following what was the first of many continued arraignments for Richard Hirschfield.

Davis Enterprise

ing Hunt and Hirschfield, many following the case believe the two men are so different in personality, intellect and social habits that they would not give each other the time of day if their paths crossed. A detective familiar with the case said Hunt and his cronies "were into drugs and ripping people off...Richard was into sexual acts."

The Hunt group spent some five years of the prime of their lives being persecuted for a crime they likely had nothing to do with – and more than a decade being considered the prime suspects by many. More than one person connected with this case on the victim/law enforcement side justified the Hunt party's ordeal by saying they deserved it because, well, they were no-goods – one family member said if a wrongful prosecution kept Hunt behind bars for a longer period, that was just fine given his violent past.

Hunt, while relieved of being cleared of involvement by Sacramento investigators, has some lingering resentment. "I don't mean to sound bitter about it, but for years I sat in prison, and my whole life was destroyed," he said. "Everybody that I know thinks I'm some kind of boogeyman. My children think so because a man of authority and a badge went over and told them."

Justice waits for the victims of any crimes committed by the Hirschfields (namely Richard) after the murders: Had Richard been apprehended in a timely fashion for these slayings, for instance, two little girls, and possibly other victims over the years, would not have been molested by him.

"People don't just wake up one day and decide to be vicious killers," noted an FBI profiler familiar with this case. "There is a maturation process that usually starts during early adolescence and progresses into adulthood. Depending on the level of organization and fantasy development, these offenders usually don't cross from fantasy or the use of consensual partners to non-consenting victims until late teens, early 20s or later. We have a saying, 'The best predictor of future behavior is past behavior.' "

The victims' families and others wonder if Richard Hirschfield is a suspect in other major crimes during the 16-plus years between the Davis murders and his 1996 arrest in Washington state. So far, authorities say, the answer is no.

"I honestly don't care," O'Mara, who oversees homicide cases, said bluntly during an October 2004 meeting with the Rigginses, some family friends and me. "It doesn't matter unless it occurred in this jurisdiction and I can charge him in this jurisdiction. If he killed 58 people in South Dakota, it doesn't matter one iota in Sacramento County."

Justice waits for a law-enforcement system that repeatedly in this case seemed more about something other than justice. Sloppiness, egos, politics, manpower shortages, petty professional jealousy and honest mistakes all got in the way. As if the longtime schism between Yolo and Sacramento counties wasn't enough, it was also apparent there was friction between prosecutors in the Sacramento District Attorney's Office and investigators in the Sheriff's Department that seemed to intensify after the DNA match.

"As far as I am concerned the time (sheriff's detectives) spent after the DNA hit investigating the case was a waste of time chasing down child-molest things and serial killer theories," said a source close to the case in the DA's office. "I kept telling them the clock is ticking – you guys need to get off your behinds and work this, and they didn't."

Hirschfield's Sacramento court-appointed attorney, Linda Parisi, a public defender and master plea bargainer known for her flamboyant, sparkly clothes and platform shoes, likes to point out that her client's DNA was found on neither the accused nor the victims, but rather something found in the van, the blanket.

She was also critical of the two-year lag between DNA match and Hirschfield's arrest. "Why is it if (Sacramento authorities) had a DNA match for two years have they waited so long to get things going? If you are accused of a crime and a key witness dies during the two-year lag, what does that do to (the defense's) ability to follow a lead? The government is not supposed to try to press an advantage, is supposed to be fair to all sides."

And just as Yolo DA Henderson appeared to have distractions prosecuting the Hunt group, Sacramento had its share during its prosecution of Hirschfield. The Sacramento District Attorney's Office's chief investigator in 2004 filed a civil suit in Sacramento County Superior Court, claiming Sacramento District Attorney Jan Scully and O'Mara ignored the investigator's complaints about alleged sexual harassment by O'Mara. According to court files, the suit claims among other things that O'Mara entered the investigator's home when she wasn't there, and left gifts and explicit phone messages, behaviors she alleges made her fear working with him. The two had a previous personal relationship that she ended in 2002, the suit said.

And a female investigator with 25 years of experience in the Sacramento County Sheriff's Department is suing Sacramento County and Homicide Bureau Supervisor Sgt. Craig Hill, contending her civil rights were violated when she was transferred out of the Homicide Bureau in February of 2002.

According to The Sacramento Bee, in a suit that was going to trial as this book went to the printer, the investigator accused Hill of regularly assigning her secretarial duties while excluding her from high-profile investigations.

She also claimed Hill, who took over as bureau supervisor in 2000, referred to her as "darling" when she asked him not to and treated her differently than her male colleagues. Attorneys for Hill said the investigator was transferred for insubordination, that she could not handle the fact that Hill was a hands-on supervisor.

Hill being a hands-on supervisor is something I can confirm as he made it very clear after the DNA match that I was not to speak to any of the current investigators in the case, just him.

And justice may always wait for Richard Joseph Hirschfield, a different kind of justice. Given that he is in his late 50s, given that he might still be on California's Death Row even had he been arrested for the murders in the early 1980s, it is more likely he will die of natural causes than by lethal injection if convicted of these murders.

"Everyone involved in this case, including Hirschfield, will likely be dead by the time he is sent to Death Row," O'Mara told Kate and Dick Riggins following Hirschfield's second court appearance. O'Mara nevertheless vowed to prosecute the case regardless of what happens. Originally planning to assign two attorneys to the case, he has opted instead to go with one, Dawn Bladet, who has some things in common with Sabrina and John: Like Sabrina, she grew up in Hawaii and she shares the same color hair as John Riggins, incidental details the families grasp as good omens at a time when good omens are needed. More important, Bladet is young — O'Mara purposely chose someone who would not be close to retirement given the long road ahead — and has a reputation for being tenacious, something that will be needed in this case. She will have her work cut out for her as she will likely be outnumbered by attorneys for Hirschfield, who gets three public defenders, one a DNA specialist.

And justice will always wait for John and Sabrina's families and friends, who have had a quarter-century wound ripped open. There may now be answers — brutal, nightmarish ones, as it turns out — but there is no closure.

"Don't ever use that word for me," Kate Riggins once noted in one of our hundreds of e-mails. Sabrina's mother, Kim, told me in 2000 that she didn't necessarily want the case solved, that she had moved on with her life, that she wasn't sure she could stomach another court adventure describing the brutal murder of a daughter she carried from the womb to the tomb. Her anguish is indescribable.

Justice waits for the Hirschfield family members who had nothing to do with this crime but whose family name is now forever tied to two awful murders. "The biggest thing we feel sorry for is the (victims') families," said Craig Hirschfield, the youngest of the six Hirschfield siblings. "Our family is kind of stuck in this now. Believe me, that's not what we're about."

The family, well known in Colusa County, feels great shame, shock even. When I called the brother between Richard and Joe in 2003, he flat-out denied being any relation, said he had no idea what I was talking about. Click.

Lana Hirschfield, Joe's widow who has since sold the property with indelible bad memories, has had her world turned upside down. She believes Joe was a reluctant participant to the killings, perhaps even was forced by Richard to take part (though prosecutors fear the defense will try to pin the murders on Joe, by using a "jackoff defense" — a crude way of suggesting that Richard merely masturbated on the blanket and that Joe did the dirty work). But Lana concedes that her husband is not without culpability — Joe's note indicating that his DNA would be found suggests he took part in Sabrina's assault — and she is sickened that something this bad happened to people this good.

"People ask me was it a drug thing? You know what? I wish it was. I wish they had killed some asshole drug dealer that nobody cares about. But it wasn't like that...And even if Joe didn't do anything, he still kept it secret all these years even when other people were being tried for it. And that is the part that hurts the most."

She said her husband never mentioned the Hunt group and she doubts Joe knew them. Lana, ironically, is a true-crime buff: She forced Joe to watch countless true-crime shows with her. "If he wanted to watch any kind of TV with me, we were watching police shows. I'm sure when there were times when somebody's second life was revealed and it tormented him...This is the sort of thing I watch on TV — I don't play it out in my living room."

Word got around quickly in Colusa County when the Hirschfields were implicated. It may be an hour's drive from Davis, but it might as well be on another planet. Colusa County may not be particularly well-educated and affluent, but it is hard-working and God-fearing, with a long-held belief in swift justice.

"I guess guilt and God both have a way of coming around and taking care of things," said a high school classmate of Joe Hirschfield.

Justice waits and justice hurts. Had I known I would have a role in getting this case reopened and possibly solved when I took on this project, I probably would have attempted a cartwheel. And while there is relief when such a baffling and tragic mystery appears solved, it has exacted a high price: I had to make some very difficult ethical choices — most involving whether to continue reporting after the DNA match was made or simply hang back until an arrest that always seemed to be just around the corner — that strained relationships with people I admire. (And I can no longer attempt cartwheels, at least not by my own volition, though the involuntary ones have a certain comedic flair.) I could write a book on writing this book. In the time I spent on it, I had just about everybody involved mad at me at one time or another and I strained some close friendships. It has by far been both the most frustrating and rewarding journalistic project in my life.

As for the principal players in this story, David Henderson continues as Yolo County district attorney, with more than two decades on the job. Notoriously aloof with the media (not unusual for a DA), he initially ignored my requests for an interview about this case, but ultimately agreed, saying he thought the publicity might spark new information leading to a possible arrest.

He was cooperative for the most part and, to his credit, gave competing agencies his blessing to talk about the case, though he became very quiet once Hirschfield was publicly named a suspect. (His office has kept close tabs on the case, namely in having an investigator or two occasionally look into whether the Hunt group has some involvement.) It was clear to me this case weighs heavily on him, and he conceded it is the most aggravating one he has ever prosecuted. He said he got threatening phone calls for about three years after he dropped the charges against the Hunt group.

Henderson was critical of the Sacramento County Sheriff's Department's handling of the case, particularly Detective Stan Reed's early dealings with David Hunt, which he feels did not go far enough, a sentiment echoed by others on the Yolo side. He is also critical of the evidence handling. "There were a number of concerns about the integrity of the evidence. We found that evidence logs did not correlate to storage records, that some items that were logged were lost, misplaced or never there and that some items such as the blanket were not stored in a locker or other location that would ensure their safety and integrity. We also found that the evidence had been stored in a variety of locations."

Reed, like a lot of his law enforcement brethren in Sacramento, including prosecutor O'Mara, is equally critical of Henderson. "David Henderson is pissed off because he doesn't get support from me and other people that David Hunt did it," Reed said.

Reed retired from homicide, and then went on to work part-time as an investigator for the Sacramento County District Attorney's Office, including working with cold-hit prosecutor Anne Marie Schubert on old cases. He candidly called the evidence oversights while he was the lead investigator on the case "embarrassing." He has kept an eye on the case since I approached him. "If there's a break in it, I'd come back and work it for free," he once said.

Reed's former boss, Ray Biondi, retired from homicide and went on to work security at Sacramento Kings home games. I found him to be a gentleman and, as it turns out, prescient about this case. And while he likely turned out to be right about the Hunt theory, he admitted the Riggins-Gonsalves case was not his or his staff's finest hour, that his department could have given the case more attention in the months and years after the murders. Ironically, he said it was his preoccupation with the Gallego murders that deflected his attention from Riggins and Gonsalves.

"It just wasn't a priority with our department at the time, with what we were trying to do. The biggest fight I had was just trying to get enough people to investigate the case."

It seems somehow fitting that shortly after the Riggins-Gonsalves case collapsed, Fred Turner took to driving a truck professionally. Tired of police work, Turner, a lover of big machines, hit the road in an 18-wheeler, where he had plenty of time to think about the case as the lonely highways unfolded in front of him. He returned to detective work when Henderson – who never lost faith in Turner despite the considerable criticism of his probe – hired him as an investigator in Yolo County's Child-Abduction Unit after the Hunt charges were dropped. He retired from the Yolo position in the summer of 2001 and returned to truck driving.

As recently as September 2004 Turner told me he still believed that the Hunt group was guilty, that Richard Hirschfield was the elusive fifth cohort, and was a mule in David Hunt's drug operation in Washington state who went by the nickname "Scooter." Scooter, never identified by his real name, was peripherally involved in Hunt's 1985 kidnap of the young Washington couple that Yolo believed is similar to John and Sabrina's abduction.

The Hirschfields, Turner maintained, "didn't act alone."

"Why kidnap a couple if you wanted a girl just to rape?"

His theory that the semen was planted appears ludicrous now, though it is also something a defense attorney may pounce on, perhaps in addition to the so-called "jackoff theory." And while Turner is looking a little Barney Fife-ish for his role in this case, he had plenty of help: had Sacramento County been more thorough in the evidence handling, had there been a determination that Sabrina had indeed been raped, had the semen stains on the blue comforter and panties not been overlooked during orders to inspect them, Fred Turner might not have been so quick to jump to conclusions. There is no shortage of oversights.

Turner speaks reverentially of Henderson. And like Henderson, Turner is critical of Sacramento County's investigation. "The Davis Police Department never should have given up the lead in the case," he said. "They should have maintained it and done all that they could have done with it."

Sacramento, meanwhile, finds Yolo's obsession with the Hunt theory comical. "With that group," one of the current investigators said derisively, "if Richard and Joe came to the door and said, 'I want to confess to this murder'

— they would have said, 'Go away.' "

During our many conversations Turner mentioned being wary of retaliation by the Hunt group, and that he has installed alarms at his home and shown pictures of the Hunt party to family members. One of them, Thompson, he need not worry about.

True to his nomadic ways, Richard Thompson bounced around in cheap motels and halfway houses after being freed when Henderson dismissed the charges in 1993. He ended up living in rural Northern California after reconciling with Valerie Thompson, his former wife whose testimony at the preliminary hearing was key in getting him bound over for trial. It didn't take Thompson long to get back into trouble: he was sent to Corcoran State Prison in 1996 for passing bad checks.

Richard Thompson died of emphysema at the age of 60 on Jan. 28, 1998. In yet another miscommunication between law enforcement agencies in this case, nobody familiar with the Riggins-Gonsalves slayings knew Thompson was seriously ill. If he had any knowledge about the murders, he took it with him to his grave. He also died without having his name cleared if he is indeed innocent, which seems likely.

"We didn't know Thompson was dying until he was already six feet under," said Haynes, who in retirement now travels the country in a motor home. "We didn't get word soon enough to interview him on his death bed."

After charges were dismissed, David Hunt was returned to federal prison in Lewisburg, Pa., where he continued serving time for the 1985 kidnapping of the Washington couple. He was later moved to a medium-security federal prison in Florence, Colo. While his sentence for kidnapping was for 35 years, he was released in August 2004 — at the age of 60. Before his release, he declined to be interviewed for this book. But after the DNA match he called me from prison on a Sunday morning in June 2003. He is wary of the media, was somewhat reluctant to talk ("I'm not sure this had the resolution you were hoping for"), and admitted being bitter and angry.

"I'd been praying for this for years," Hunt said of the DNA match. "I didn't really expect it. I hoped for it. I'm not going to pretend like I am some innocent person when I was younger. I know exactly what I was. But I never did any of that stuff."

Hunt said he quit communicating with Gallego after he learned his half-brother was a killer. He called Henderson a "lying dog." Turner, Hunt contended, was primarily motivated by his admitted desire to write a book on the case.

While Hunt declined to discuss Hirschfield or any of the new developments specifically with me, he did address some of the lingering questions about the weekend of Dec. 20, 1980. As for confusing Carson City with Las Vegas, Hunt said he was "high all the time" and that, when pressed to recall the weekend when approached by authorities "one day ran into the other."

"We weren't figuring we had to keep track of where we were," he explained.

He added that he was wanted in California for busting Thompson out of San Quentin, and the notion of returning to the state didn't make sense under any circumstances. "What the hell would we be doing coming back into California? We were armed criminals and we were doing what armed criminals would be doing. California was the last place in the world that we were going to try to go to."

While he declined to discuss his specific activities the night of Dec. 20, 1980, Hunt said that he has no recollection of the "family business" comment, and is still angry that he "didn't have my trial where I got to say what I wanted to say." He said being a suspect in the murders added time to his prison term, which he claimed he spent, among other things, writing a book and learning heating and air conditioning repair. He was reportedly a well-behaved prisoner, which, perhaps along with cooperating with detectives in this case, led to his early parole on Aug. 25, 2004, to a halfway house in the Seattle area.

He never made it. Not even close. Nada.

Despite being in his 60s, Hunt has apparently turned into a sort of geriatric Jesse James. He returned to his outlaw ways the moment he got a whiff of freedom shortly after being interviewed by Yolo detectives who apparently were still trying to connect him to the Davis killings. According to a federal agent whose job is tracking down fugitives, Hunt skipped an unescorted bus furlough from Colorado to Seattle, and instead fled to Mexico on Aug. 28, 2004. His relationship with Suellen apparently over by this time, Hunt was aided by a lonely 72-year-old widow who wrote to him while he was in prison. Authorities say he smooth-talked the woman into liquidating some $70,000 of her life savings to bankroll his post-prison plans. Hunt and the woman, who has no criminal record, somehow made it across the border, where Hunt is suspected of being a leader in a drug ring with other U.S. ex-cons and escapees he met in prison. The agent believes Hunt's gang in Mexico includes several armed and dangerous men. One ex-con who planned to join the group

David Hunt in Mexico in November 2004.

was killed in a shootout with police in Minnesota after a robbery.

Hunt, the federal agent said, "met this other woman and manipulated her and she cashed a bunch of her retirement and they were going to live in a trailer and RV park when he got out of a halfway house.

"When the (Yolo) homicide detectives went to visit him, his plans changed and he had this woman pick him up and boogie down to Mexico, which leads me to believe he is a little nervous about the (Davis) double-homicide."

Perhaps. Or maybe old habits, like old outlaws, die hard. Maybe Hunt fled to Mexico with his older version of Suellen because, as his lengthy criminal record indicates, life as a law-abiding citizen, where any advantages save AARP discounts would be hard to come by, simply isn't something he is capable of, interested in or excited by. Having Yolo still interested in him despite DNA evidence and a suicide strongly pointing to other culprits probably didn't give him much confidence to hang around, either. "I think he was planning this thing for several years," the federal agent said of the Mexican getaway. "The Yolo interview just sent him down south early."

The agent noted that Hunt is suspected of interacting with "a group of guys who all knew each other and their claim to fame is they all committed a homicide." The agent went so far as to speculate that Hunt may actually have fabricated stories about committing the Davis killings to impress his fellow outlaws in Mexico. He certainly has enough information from his lengthy prosecution to do so.

Hunt was captured on July 1, 2005, in Chapala, Mexico. He did not go down easily, fleeing from the building he was in and being tackled by authorities. The agent in charge of tracking him down said the Federal Bureau of Prisons did not inform his office of Hunt's escape until some three months after it occurred.

Though he enjoyed a good escape as much as his half-brother, there is no fear of further Gerald Gallego escapes because he died July 18, 2002, of rectal cancer in a prison hospital on Nevada's Death Row. I requested an interview months before he died and got no reply. Similar requests of Richard Hirschfield have been declined.

Suellen has apparently had less drama. After Henderson dropped the murder charges against her, she returned to her parents' upscale house in the Bay Area, where she takes care of her ailing mother. She said she and Hunt are divorced, though they were, at least while he was still in prison, in regular contact. She also keeps in periodic contact with Lainer. She said her arrest and incarceration ruined any chance of holding a job.

I had several phone conversations with Suellen. At first she agreed to sit down for an interview, then declined after she heard that I had mentioned during a radio interview in 2001 that I hadn't eliminated the Hunt party as the possible culprits (at the time I was leaning toward their involvement). Talking about the case, she told me, is what got her in trouble in the first place.

"Every time I opened my mouth, the people that are involved in the legal system twisted it around and ruined my life more," she said prior to the DNA match. "I'd give anything I have to make this something that could be solved so that I didn't feel like there were people out there who think I have killed their children. It is just an awful, horrible thing to live with."

Suellen did address the one burning question I had for her: How could you "forget" where you were married and when?

"If you were to ask me that in — what year? 1980? — if I was in Las Vegas, I probably wouldn't have thought so," she said in a husky voice. "But that's where (Hunt and Thompson) originally wanted me to meet them, so when asked years later that's basically what's in my head — and David's, too, that we had gone to Las Vegas."

I told Suellen that married people sometimes have trouble recalling when they got married. But where? A woman forgetting where? Suellen replied that at the time she did not pay much attention to where she was, was often sleeping on the floor of vans while a passenger, and was ignorant about Nevada geography.

"I now, thanks to Turner and everybody, do know the difference in how large Nevada is...I didn't know the difference then. I have no sense of direction, no sense of anything like that, never have. I just get maps from AAA and follow them. I had no idea whether (Carson City and Las Vegas) were very far away or close."

We talked again after the DNA match. She said she was "quite relieved" by the news, characterized Turner as a "sleaze bucket," said she is not as bitter as she once was, and feels for the victims' families. "What happened to me due to my associations with people is really my own doing, so you don't have to feel sorry for me," she said. "But you really do need to feel sorry for the Riggins and Gonsalves families. Because if Turner hadn't had his desires to write a book and Henderson hadn't had his desires to make sure his re-election didn't look good — and I don't know about (Yolo investigator) Haynes. Haynes I will never understand — if that hadn't been the case, those families would not have been put through that torture for no reason."

Lainer, the lone Hunt party member who agreed to be interviewed prior to the match, talked to me in 2002 in the modest apartment he shares with his wife and stepdaughter in Hayward, where he continues to work as a truck driver and tries to stay off drugs. He said that when confronted by Turner, he believed the other three suspects were in fact guilty.

"At the beginning I thought, these guys did this, because the way the police presented it, it seems as though they did. But the more I reviewed the discovery and the transcripts, the more doubtful I was about their guilt...I know David, and he does not hurt women."

Lainer's inability to provide an alibi for his whereabouts on Dec. 20, 1980, is one of the things that led to his arrest. Prior to the DNA match, he said he was "hustling pain pills" by seeking emergency dental care at Dominican Hospital in Santa Cruz that afternoon, and that Turner never bothered checking it out. Turner countered that Santa Cruz is close enough to Davis for Lainer to have driven to the Lucky shopping center that fateful night.

Besides, Turner added skeptically of the dental visit, "that would make the third or fourth alibi" for Lainer.

Though known to be tightly wound, Lainer kept his cool when we talked prior to the cold hit. That is, until he learned that Turner thought the blanket semen was planted. "They're not going to admit they are wrong, man, ever! What about the semen on the panties, then? How did that get there? Jesus Christ, it just goes on and on, man."

The Hunt group was contacted – and cleared – by the Sacramento investigators in June of 2003. Lainer declined to be interviewed by them because of what happened the first time. Suellen cooperated. David Hunt ultimately did as well, though it is unclear what, if anything he said to Yolo investigators before fleeing to Mexico – or what they said to him.

After the charges were dropped in 1992, Lainer, Thompson and Suellen filed lawsuits against Henderson, Turner, Haynes, informant and apparent liar Ray Lopez, Yolo County and the city of Davis claiming emotional distress, false arrest, wrongful searches, and illegal interrogation, among other things. None of the lawsuits was successful: Thompson dropped his not long after he filed it, Lainer's was tossed when he failed to come up with a filing fee, and an appellate court dismissed Suellen's. Suellen, the onetime law student, acted as her own attorney, and did a good job, says Bruce Kilday, the attorney hired by Yolo County to defend the suit. "She's very, very smart," he said.

Suellen also said in a deposition in her lawsuit that she was with Hunt Dec. 20 through Dec. 21, 1980. In the same deposition, she was questioned about how she could confuse Las Vegas with Carson City:

Q: "In 1980, you planned to go to Las Vegas but that plan was changed by you and David, and even you had to go to the extent of looking at a map yourself to find where Carson City was and then planning your own course to Carson City; is that correct?"

Suellen: "Correct."

Q: "So you're saying that even though you did that, even though you had obtained the map guidance from AAA to get to Las Vegas, were told to change it to Carson City, had to find Carson City on your own, had to determine your own route to Carson City and then, indeed to drive to Carson City in the middle of the night, you had forgotten by 1987 that you had actually gone to Carson City?"

Suellen: "Correct."

Lainer said he was offered $40,000 to settle the lawsuit, and that he declined, but said he would have settled for $100,000. But, he said, it wasn't money so much that he was after. "An apology would have made it all go away," he said, shaking his head.

The ravine where John and Sabrina were found is now occupied by the Folsom Automall, an expansive group of car dealerships that serve as a reminder of just how much the greater Sacramento region has grown since the slayings. There is something so...impersonal about it all.

I drove out there on Dec. 20, 2000 – the 20th anniversary of the murders, and the most emotional day for me. I had a hard time finding the ravine.

Hopelessly lost, I ran into a robust gent, about 65, who, clad in a wet suit, was puffing on a rope of a cigar after a swim in nearby Lake Natoma. Clutching a photocopy of a Sacramento Bee clipping from 1980 that showed a simple locator map of the area ("BODIES," the map says next to a circled X), I asked him if he recalled the murders as the clipping flapped in the breeze. "Oh, yes," he said. "I had just moved here then. Awful it was."

The man squinted at the map, then raised a latex-covered arm and pointed toward the ravine. "Over there is where they found 'em, in what used to be a brushy area with lots of trees," he noted. Then he added a comment that I thought summed up a lot of how the region has changed since the murders: "See, they didn't have all that auto mall shit then."

(In yet another coincidence to this case, some of Richard Hirschfield's criminal records were, prior to the DNA match, stored in a California Department of Corrections facility on Aerojet Road in Sacramento, the same road off which John and Sabrina's bodies were found.)

Sabrina's condominium complex, the likely abduction site, looks much the same as it did in 1980 – and remains a dark, isolated place at night, spooky still. The Davis shopping center where the couple were thought by many to be abducted is laid out much the same as it was in 1980. By Davis standards, this is a sprawling shopping center with myriad entrances, breezeways and side entrances.

With the exception of a Baskin-Robbins Ice Cream store that still anchors one of the breezeways the killers are suspected of using, and the Ding How Chinese restaurant, almost all of the businesses that were here in 1980 are gone, their spaces now occupied by something else. The Lucky supermarket where John and Sabrina may have bought the ice cream is now an Albertson's.

As with the ravine, I visited the shopping center on the 20th anniversary of John and Sabrina's death. My wife and I on this night ate at Ding How, a popular Davis Chinese restaurant that was in the shopping center in 1980

— an impressive feat given Davis' restaurant turnover rate. It had switched locations to the former Chandelier restaurant, where one witness reported seeing Sabrina and John eyeballing a menu outside 20 years earlier.

The last thing we did before heading back to Sacramento is snap open a couple of fortune cookies. Normally I shrug off fortunes as feel-good hokum, but on this night, this most dubious of Davis anniversaries marked by little more than a clear, inky sky as opposed to the ominous fog two decades hence, mine had an ironic twist. *"You believe,"* the thin strip of pink paper reads, *"in the goodness of mankind."*

28
Legacy

Kim Eichorn

"A little love and affection
in everything you do
will make the world a better place
with or without you"

— Neil Young

Strange what the murder of a family member can do to you, even a quarter of a century later. Kate Riggins is repulsed by the sight of duct tape ("knowing that Sabrina and John were bound by the tape causes me to me to feel ill and so helpless"), and has nightmares that her son is still alive, lying in that cold, dark ditch. If her surviving children are late showing up somewhere, panic sets in. And John's father, Dick? Hard to say. To this day he can't talk about it. "Dick has great problems with my discussing what happened on Dec. 20, 1980. He only sees in his mind his son being bound, gagged, with his throat slashed, bleeding to death and not being able to save him," Kate explained.

The Rigginses are now retired — though busy in volunteer circles — and living on the Central California Coast in a simple bungalow with a stunningly spectacular view of the Pacific Ocean. Dec. 20 is a bittersweet day: Both the anniversary of their marriage and the murder of their first child. There are still awkward moments with new acquaintances. When asked how many children they have, it's usually easier to change the subject.

Many a night Kate Riggins has sat in the front room of her heavenly piece of real estate, the moon glimmering over the ocean outside, only to have her picture-postcard setting shattered when her thoughts drift to the torturous mystery of just who killed her son and why. She and Dick, both nattily attired — Dick in his trademark bow tie, Kate in an elegant blue dress, attended Hirschfield's second court hearing in Sacramento. Like the Gonsalveses at the previous hearing, they were calm and poised. Class acts.

Sabrina's parents split their time between their native Hawaii and Southern California, the latter near Andrea's upscale Southern California home she shares with her veterinarian husband and five children. Andrea's birthday is on the day her sister was found dead. Her family tried to throw her a surprise birthday party in her mid-30s. "I was a wreck," she said.

Little things that linger from two decades ago eat at you, make you contrite even though they shouldn't. Sabrina's parents, for example, feel guilty that they didn't view her body at the funeral home.

"And we've never gotten rid of that. It is something we will take to our grave," Kim Gonsalves said, sobbing. "We both regret it. I had told them what to put on her. I had a rosary put in her casket with her but I never went and looked at her. They told us she had damage done to her face. And that just killed me, and I didn't want to see her face. And now I am so angry that I didn't look."

When your child is murdered you are suddenly part of a club that nobody wants to join. In this environment, one can actually take solace in some ways: Both families said that unlike some murdered children they knew of, at least John and Sabrina suffered for a relatively short time. And their bodies were recovered, something that many parents of murdered children are still waiting for.

There isn't a day that goes by that John and Sabrina aren't missed, thought about, prayed for. And while the deaths have left a wound that will never heal, both families have held together remarkably well, whether it be through religion, each other, or sheer determination. No divorce, no apparent problems. The surviving siblings are happy and well-adjusted, though Carrie Riggins Mack, and her musician-husband, Todd, were dealt a devastating blow in 2002 when journalist Daniel Pearl, a good friend who played in Todd Mack's band, was murdered in Pakistan. Carrie has now endured two kidnapping-murders of a loved one that have horrific parallels. If that's not enough, she was also listed as deceased in the program for her Davis High 20th reunion, perhaps mistaken for her brother. She is very much alive, a working mom and one of the more vibrant, candid people I interviewed.

Both sets of parents have been active in support groups for parents of murdered or missing children. "I was determined whoever destroyed John and Sabrina was not going to destroy our family," Kate Riggins maintained.

The Gonsalveses feel the same way.

"If Sabrina thought in any way that this murder hurt us or broke us up or ruined any relationships or in any way held us back," said Andrea, "she would be very, very upset with us. We needed to do a good job carrying on for her."

The families, who rarely set foot in Davis anymore, keep in touch and occasionally visit each other. Neither blames the other for what happened. "There was never any 'She shouldn't have been with him, that reckless kid,' " Kate Riggins observed. "Or vice versa. So we didn't have any negative feelings like that. We just had this great sorrow together."

There was, however, some lingering resentment among some Gonsalves family members over how the murders were initially handled. The day I spent interviewing the Gonsalveses in person in 2000, I got an earful about how, in their opinion, Andrea bore the brunt of dealing with detectives, the community and the media in the months following the murders. The Gonsalveses, the only family to attend Hunt court proceedings, also felt that they were not given enough credit or say in how the considerable charitable funds were raised or would be spent, and that they were the forgotten outsiders over time. (The resentment seemed to have long dissipated when I met with both sets of parents in Davis in 2004 at the funeral of mutual friend Dr. Paul Lipscomb.)

Both sets of parents are firm believers in the death penalty, are understandably much behind DNA testing (including a voter-approved measure expanding California's DNA database to all suspected felons regardless of whether they are convicted), think prisoners have it too easy, and are advocates of victims' rights. One of the documents Kate Riggins sent to me, just before the DNA match, was a copy of John's death certificate, on which she had affixed a hand-written Post-It note reading, "Whoever did this to my son should not be allowed to live!"

Just about every conversation I had or e-mail I got from George Gonsalves mentioned the death penalty.

The loss of John Riggins and Sabrina Gonsalves is immeasurable. Given their history of high achievement, their solid family backgrounds, their concern for children and their community, it follows that they would have been high-achieving contributors whether they stayed together – which seems likely – or went their separate ways.

But if their lives were too short, their legacy endures. Since their deaths, a vast amount has been done in Sabrina and John's names:

— A memorial footbridge over a creek in rural Mendocino County was built in a stretch of virgin redwoods by friends of John and Sabrina in the spring of 1981.

— Sabrina's high school in Germany dedicated its 1981 yearbook to her.

— In 1982 a plaque was placed near a tree that was planted in John and Sabrina's memory in the UC Davis Arboretum, one of many trees that have been planted in the couple's memory.

— A bench in John's name was dedicated at the UC Davis soccer field, and "most-inspirational" athletic awards bear his name.

— An asteroid named "Sabrina-John" – the 4,160th known asteroid – was named for the couple after it was discovered by Sabrina's brother-in-law, Carlos Atallah. "Hurtling through space on its eternal journey, this asteroid symbolizes the endurance of their love," the dedication says.

— Best known among the many tributes was the Warm Remembrance

Festival. Using money donated to a fund in the couple's name, the city of Davis in 1981 launched a festival for families and children in Davis' Central Park. The popular festival was held every August until the mid-1990s. It lasted almost as long as John and Sabrina's lives.

— A water slide and baseball fence. After the Warm Remembrance Festival was discontinued, the remaining funds — said to total near $10,000 — were used toward the purchase of a double-flume water slide at Davis Community Pool, and a baseball fence for the Davis High baseball diamond on which John played.

— For years the rocks on the levee adjacent to the Yolo Causeway spelled out "YOU'RE MISSED, JOHN & SABRINA" every Dec. 20. Nobody knows for sure who put them there, though the rumor is it was John's soccer teammates.

— Sabrina's dog, Shannon, had puppies, one of which, Skyla, was given to the Rigginses and was Robert Riggins' loyal sidekick for years. Skyla was so beloved that, after she died, her ashes were scattered in the same place as John's.

— Perhaps the most enduring tribute to John and Sabrina can be found in...Young John and Sabrina.

John Riggins Mack was born in 2000 and is Carrie and Todd Mack's second child and first son. His smile is similar to his namesake uncle's and he shares John's high energy, if not his red hair. He is the spitting image of grandfather Richard/Dick Riggins, so much so that his nickname is "Little Richard." "I would have loved it if he had red hair, but he's towheaded," Carrie said, adding that naming her son John was a "wonderfully easy" decision. "But he does have (his late uncle's) blue eyes."

Sabrina Marie Rosenstein is the first-born child to Andrea Gonsalves Rosenstein. Like Sabrina, she is pretty and quiet, athletic and poised. She planned on attending UC Davis at one time.

I didn't have to ask this Sabrina what it's like being named after the aunt she never met. She took care of that herself in a poignant school essay she wrote when she was 14 and in the ninth grade.

What's in a Name?

How do I feel about naming children for people who have died?

The question is central to my life and brings me to a special memory – standing in Punchbowl Memorial Cemetery – a national monument on a beautiful day in paradise. I am looking down. The sweet, warm Hawaiian air wraps around me. The air was thick with feelings, and experiences of death, life, and goodness, all combined with joy and pain.

The lush bright green grass under my feet, well-kept grass, was offering happiness and showing life.

Bright flowers are happy gifts, were tokens of love and remembrance. As I look down at the cold, hard slab, for a moment I pause; wait, that's my name!

Then I remember, it is also <u>her</u> name. The dates glare at me. Such a short distance between them, 18 years. That's a small number. What can one unprepared person experience in 18 years? The voices of my family bring me back. Talking to her, sharing, loving, and missing her.

I feel an eerie connection to the person they are talking to. A closeness I can't explain, over a name, yet also a distance from being unacquainted. It's amazing how a name can make me feel.

The murder of Sabrina and John profoundly impacted their families, friends, the University of Davis and the city of Davis.

So much of their lives were away all of a sudden.

It was an unforgettable tragedy. My mother also attended UC

Davis and shared a small apartment with Sabrina, her little sister.

She was very brave and showed tremendous courage going back to live in the apartment alone after her sister's kidnap and murder.

My mother showed determination and courage when she helped police in their efforts to solve the murder of her little sister.

Looking for her own personal resolution to the violent, unsolved murder of her younger sister, my mother decided to dedicate her first child to her sister who was denied a chance to have her own children.

My mother was set and determined to name her first daughter Sabrina, despite others' opinions. My mother told (my father) before they talked of marriage that she planned on naming her first daughter Sabrina. This shows just how important this was to my mother.

I think it was also brave of her to put their relationship at risk to make her dream of commemorating her little sister real. People thought naming me Sabrina was either terrible or special.

My mother's professor in child psychology, her mentor, put her heart at ease when she told my mother that Pablo Picasso was the sixth child named Pablo – all the others died. She showed great wisdom when she told my mother that the child called Sabrina will be graced by the love the family has for her sister Sabrina.

My mother went through much pain and showed great strength

when she named me Sabrina.

Well, I've been named Sabrina and looking back this has had a big impact on my life. I was named after someone who was deeply loved by my family. I feel a sad, deep loss for myself, who never got to meet this special person. Part of me is worried I won't succeed to my full potential. Another part of me is worried I won't succeed to live as full a life as Sabrina would have, or I may not succeed to my full potential. Another part of me is very proud of my mother and happy to be named after her beloved little sister. However, I was also named after someone who was violently murdered. I suppose some people would become superstitious of this discovery. Fortunately, I am a very pragmatic person. I don't believe that anything will happen to me because of my name. I feel that it is a privilege to be named after such a special person.

I have been asked by many different people if I would name one of my children after one of my sisters if one of them died. One of the people who asked me this question was my mother. I honestly don't know the answer to that question. I don't believe that anyone can answer that question. I don't believe that anyone can answer that question without having experienced the death of a close person. I have never experienced the death of anyone close to me. I don't see how being named after someone who died (even violently) is a bad thing at all. I don't believe it is "cursing" the child. I think it is a good thing to be living for someone.

It gives me a whole closeness to a person I never got to meet. It also makes me feel special and like I have a closer bond with my family.

I hope I never lose a loved one.

— Sabrina Marie Rosenstein

Who's Who

Sabrina Gonsalves: Murdered, Dec. 20, 1980.

John Riggins: Murdered, Dec. 20, 1980.

Bob Bell: Sacramento County homicide detective.

Lt. Ray Biondi: Former head of Sacramento County Homicide Bureau.

Gerald Gallego: Serial killer/David Hunt's half-brother.

George and Kim Gonsalves: Sabrina's parents.

Andrea (Gonsalves) Rosenstein: Sabrina's sister/roommate.

Terese (Gonsalves) Atallah: Sabrina's oldest sister (hosted surprise birthday party for Andrea on Dec. 20, 1980).

Stephen Gonsalves: Sabrina's brother.

John Haynes: Investigator, Yolo County district attorney's office who pursued Hunt party.

David Henderson: Yolo County district attorney.

Sgt. Craig Hill: Current head of the Sacramento County Homicide Bureau.

Richard J. Hirschfield: Murder suspect linked by DNA to the killings in 2002.

Joseph Hirschfield: Richard's younger brother who committed suicide in 2002 after being confronted about the murders.

David Hunt: Gallego's half-brother, charged with Riggins-Gonsalves murders, November 1989.

Suellen Hunt: Hunt's wife, charged with Riggins-Gonsalves murders, November 1989.

Doug Lainer: Hunt/Richard Thompson prison buddy, charged with Riggins-Gonsalves murders in 1990 after refusing to testify.

Bill Lansing: Key Yolo witness; was with Hunt party night of the killings.

Judge Rudolph Loncke: Presided over Hunt party's preliminary hearing.

*Ray Lopez: Informant who fingered Hunt party in Davis killings.

John O'Mara: Sacramento deputy district attorney who declined to prosecute the Hunt party, but has vowed to prosecute Richard Hirschfield.

Linda Parisi: Richard Hirschfield's attorney.

Dr. Richard and Kate Riggins: John's parents.

Carrie and Robert Riggins: John's siblings.

Mark Safarik: Davis police detective, now an FBI profiler.

Anne Marie Schubert: Sacramento deputy district attorney in charge of DNA "cold hit" program.

Faye Springer: Trace evidence expert.

Richard Thompson: Hunt's crime partner, charged with Riggins-Gonsalves murders, November 1989.

---

*The names of some people in this book have been changed. Such names are denoted by an asterisk (*) the first time each appears in the book.

Chronology

1975

April 30
Richard Hirschfield breaks into Mountain View apartment, ties up sisters and younger sister's boyfriend, sexually assaults sisters and rifles apartment.

May 5
Richard Hirschfield is arrested after he is found prowling in Sunnyvale apartment complex.

Various dates
Richard Hirschfield and David Hunt both in the Santa Clara County Jail (on separate occasions) and the California Medical Facility (CMF) in Vacaville, possibly at the same time.

1980

Summer
John Riggins and Sabrina Gonsalves start dating.

July 2
Richard Hirschfield paroled from the CMF, moves in with younger brother Joe.

Oct. 14
David Hunt paroled from San Quentin, moves in with Suellen in Menlo Park.

Nov. 2
CSU Sacramento sweethearts Mary Beth Sowers and Craig Miller are murdered by Gerald Gallego with help of his wife, Charlene.

Nov. 4
David Hunt makes "Anything I can do?" call to Charlene's mother.

Nov. 14
Gallegos arrested in Nebraska.

Nov. 24
Hunt helps break Richard Thompson out of San Quentin.

Dec. 2
Gallegos jailed in Sacramento.

Dec. 15
Doug Lainer paroled from San Quentin, is picked up by Suellen.

Dec. 18
"Blood ritual" among Richard and Valerie Thompson and David Hunt at Phoenix, Ariz. apartment.

Dec. 19
Suellen gives Lainer $1,000 check (she also gives a $1,400 check to another ex-con with no suspected involvement in the case).

Dec. 20
7 a.m. Hunt and Thompsons and Bill Lansing arrive at Carson City Motel 6, where they meet Suellen, who arrives in rental van with daughter and pets.

1:30 to 2 p.m. David and Suellen Hunt's "marriage."

Late afternoon/early evening Lansing is dropped off at casino, told "we have family business" by David Hunt.

8:30 p.m. Last definitive sighting of John and Sabrina, leaving "Nutcracker" production in Davis.

8:30 to 9 p.m. Lucky employee says he saw John and Sabrina in the store. Witnesses say they saw two suspicious-looking men in shopping center breezeway.

8:45 to 11 p.m. Riggins' van sightings in Davis, along Yolo Causeway and at murder site.

About 10 p.m. Riggins' van seen backing up to ravine.

10 to 11 p.m. Witness sees van in front of Rudy's Hideaway with door open, motor running and lights on. Another witness sees a suspicious man walking on Folsom Boulevard. A couple coming out of Rudy's see two suspicious men walking out of a field.

Dec. 21

Midnight to 9 a.m. Hunt group departs Carson City for Phoenix, Ariz.

7:30 a.m. John and Sabrina declared missing by families.

9 a.m. Man with bloody T-shirt seen picked up by a second man not far from ravine.

Evening Victims' families descend on Davis Police Department, demand search.

Dec. 22

12:07 a.m. Case classified as a kidnapping, state and federal agencies alerted.

8 a.m. Riggins' van found.

11:10 a.m. Bodies found.

3:30 p.m. John's autopsy.

4 p.m. Sabrina's autopsy.

Dec. 24
A Sacramento County Jail inmate tells authorities he believes David Hunt committed copycat killing.

Dec. 29
Gerald Gallego files discovery motion seeking information on Riggins-Gonsalves murders.

1981

Date unknown
Richard and Joe Hirschfield likely move to Arbuckle (Colusa County).

January
Informant Ray Lopez tells authorities David Hunt committed the murders.

Feb. 19
Hunt arrested in Chico, Calif., for Thompson escape. Suellen is with him.

March 4
Hunt, in jail in Sacramento for Thompson escape, is interviewed by Detective Stan Reed about the murders, denies any involvement, but also would not say where he was on Dec. 20, 1980.

Oct. 19
Richard Hirschfield is required to register in Williams — about 50 miles from Davis — as a convicted sex offender for 1975 home-invasion rape.

1982

April 6
Detective Reed interviews Hunt by phone about the murders. Hunt says he has no recollection of his whereabouts on Dec. 20, 1980.

July
Hunt freed from jail for lack of evidence in Thompson escape.

1983

Date unknown
Joseph Hirschfield moves to Oregon.

July 27
Richard Hirschfield arrested but not prosecuted on suspicion of brandishing a weapon in Willows, Calif.

1985

June 22
Hunt arrested at Ft. Lewis, Wash., for kidnapping a young couple.
He is sentenced to 35 years in federal prison.

1987

March 31
Davis Police Detective Fred Turner begins his investigation,
locates David Hunt.

May 28
Richard Thompson paroled to Los Angeles after serving time for 1980
prison escape.

July 15-20
Informant Ray Lopez meets with Richard Thompson in Los Angeles hotel,
claims he got a full confession on murders, records "duct tape" comment.

July 27
Thompson flees Hotel Cecil in Los Angeles after finding police phone number in informant Lopez's pocket.

1989

Nov. 14
The Hunts and Richard Thompson arrested on suspicion
of murdering John and Sabrina.

1990

May 29
Douglas Lainer arrested on suspicion of murdering John and Sabrina.

1992

Richard Hirschfield living in Arcata, Calif.

1993

Jan. 29
Murder charges dropped against the Hunt party. Some 20 associates
checked for DNA. None match.

1996

Summer
Richard Hirschfield arrested for child molestation in Washington state.

2002

June 21
Joel Davis brings case to the attention of Sacramento County District
Attorney's Office; office subsequently launches its own investigation.

August 27
"Cold hit" made on blanket semen, Sacramento County launches new
probe, freezes Joel Davis, Yolo County and District Attorney David Henderson out.

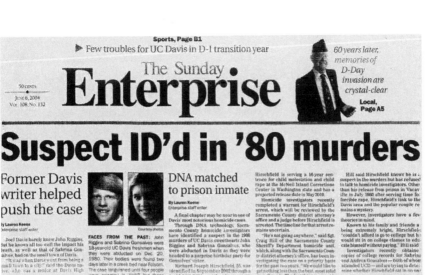

The Davis Enterprise on June 6, 2004, broke the story of the Richard Hirschfield DNA match.

September/October
Yolo and Sacramento counties conduct counter-investigations.

Nov. 19
Richard Hirschfield, in custody, confronted with DNA evidence, declines to speak to detectives, asks for an attorney.

Nov. 21
Joseph J. Hirschfield commits suicide the day after being confronted about the murders.

2004

June 6
Richard Hirschfield publicly named a suspect for the first time by The Davis Enterprise.

Aug.25
After 20 years behind bars, David Hunt is paroled from federal prison in Colorado and assigned to a halfway house in Seattle. He instead flees to Mexico with female pen pal and her life's savings on Aug.28, after being interviewed by Yolo County detectives about the Davis case. After resuming his outlaw lifestlyle, he is caputred July 1, 2005, in Chapala, Mexico.

September
Richard Hirschfield fights extradition to Sacramento.

Sept. 25
Richard Hirschfield arrested, lodged in Sacramento County Jail, where he soon is pummeled by other inmates over use of a payphone.

Sept. 27
The first of several arraignments for Richard Hirschfield where he and his attorney asked for a continuance rather than enter a plea. As of the summer of 2005, Hirschfield had yet to enter a plea.**

**Visit www.justicewaits.com for updates on this case.

Thanks!

A lot of people made this book possible, chief among them my wife, Kelly, and the families of John and Sabrina. I am especially indebted to George Gonsalves and Andrea Gonsalves Rosenstein for all they did on behalf of their family, and to Kate Riggins for her interest and amazing support for the duration of this project. And I could not have finished this book without John Hershey, who was every bit my co-pilot in the crucial final months. A huge thank-you to graphic artist extraordinaire Jay Leek, who handled layout and design, including designing the one thing everyone seems to like — the cover.

And this book would have been next to impossible if not for Debbie Davis and The Davis Enterprise.

I also appreciate the cooperation of many of the key people in this story: Many of the central players were asked many tough questions — and sometimes even responded, and were especially helpful when the case was cold. There are some sources here who I wish I could thank publicly, but then they wouldn't be sources. So thanks...

Others to whom I am indebted: My family and in-laws; Jeff Aberbach; Dan Ariola; Jane Beauchamp; Rod Beede; Ryan Bright and ADA workers/ upholders everywhere; Kathy Brown and Laurie Houghton of Sheridan Books, Inc.; Doug Buchanan; the California First Amendment Coalition and the First Amendment itself; The Chico Club; The Chumps; Robert Cooper; Joe Davidson; Anna Davis; Kathi Denny; Scott Donald; Bob Dunning; Leo and Mary Kay Edson; Kim Eichorn; Jim Ewert; Wendy Fantozzi; David and Lisa Forster; Dan Fost; Terry Francke and Californians Aware; Dr. Andy and Judy Gabor; Susan Gorsch; Dr. Keith Grote and family; Gary Harmor; Rachel Heffner; Scott Hill; Lana Hirschfield; Lauren Keene; Bruce Kilday; Lisa Ladd-Wilson; Phyllis Lipscomb; Tom Newton; the Parkinson Foundation of Northern California, Sacramento; Gary Pruitt; Carolyn Ralston; the River Park Neighborhood Association; Tonya Rizzo; Robyn Rutger; Frances Sackett; The Sacramento Bee; the Sacramento Business Journal; the Sacramento News & Review; Elisabeth Sherwin; Joel and Susan Swift; Dr. Vicki

L. Wheelock; Charles Winkler and the Times-Standard, Eureka; Winnie; Pete Winterling; Joe Wirt; Dr. Robert and Joyce Wisner; Vince Young; and Michael J. Fox. I am a lucky man...